WILD RIDE

*How Coffee, Concealer, and
Conversations with God became
The Faith Journey of a Caregiver*

A Journal, A Blog, An Unintentional Book Series

CONSTANCE MURRAY

WESTBOW
P R E S S®
A DIVISION OF THOMAS NELSON
& ZONDERVAN

WestBow Press books may be ordered through booksellers or by contacting:

WestBow Press
A Division of Thomas Nelson & Zondervan
1663 Liberty Drive
Bloomington, IN 47403
www.westbowpress.com
844-714-3454

Interior Image Credit: Constance Murray

ISBN: 979-8-3850-3760-5 (sc)
ISBN: 979-8-3850-3761-2 (e)

Print information available on the last page.

WestBow Press rev. date: 01/20/2025

CONTENTS

PREFACE

This book didn't begin as a book. It began as a personal journal, and a series of social media posts and updates about my late husband Robert James Murray, Jr. (Robb) and his cancer treatments. It started off as a closed FB group called *Robb Murray's Wild Ride* that was mostly family and close friends, but quickly grew to anyone who was willing to follow his journey and pray for him and our family. It turned into a faith journey for me – the caregiver. God used our circumstances to draw us nearer to Him and to grow my relationship with Him in ways I never dreamed possible. This is the story of the Wild Ride of my personal faith journey.

I pray that in reading about my faith journey, God opens your eyes to see Him and opens your heart to hear His voice and feel His guidance. He wants a relationship with you. He loves you.

The bulk of this book was written in doctor's office waiting rooms, on the chemotherapy infusion unit, in hospital rooms, and surgical waiting areas. The compilation and final touches were done in the quiet of my home while praying for God's guidance to say the things He wants me to say. I pray He is pleased with the final product, and I pray that you are blessed reading how God took the most terrifying circumstances and gave us everything we *needed* precisely when we needed it (not necessarily everything we *wanted* when we wanted it).

I am often blunt and many times write like I am having a conversation with you the reader. Don't expect everything to be 'proper' and grammatically correct cause that ain't happen'n.

ACKNOWLEDGEMENT

Thank you to all those who were there for me – sometimes or all the time. God put the right people in my life when I needed them. I know He will continue to guide me.

A special thank you to Lynn Saia and Pamela Farrow Shannon, my emotional and spiritual support during the worst time of my life. Thank you to Melissa Kehm for proof editing and being my first 'outside of the circle' reader. Thank you to Lynn Saia for all her input. Without her perspective, this book would never have come to completion.

Prayer quilt given to Robb when he was first diagnosed.

ACKNOWLEDGEMENT

Prayer quilt given to Robb when he was first diagnosed.

THE WILD RIDE

According to dictionary.com a vow is a noun meaning a solemn promise, pledge, or personal commitment; an earnest declaration; a solemn promise made to a deity committing oneself to an act, service, or condition.

On May 10, 1986, we stood before our families and God and we recited our vows. I took a vow. I made a solemn promise and committed myself to the conditions in our vows. I meant those words, but I honestly had no idea just how those conditions would play out and how my commitment to my husband would be tested.

I Constance take you Robert to be my lawfully wedded husband. To have and to hold from this day forward, for better or for worse, for richer, for poorer, in sickness and in health, to love and to cherish, forsaking all others, until death do us part.

We knew there would be 'worse' and 'poorer'. We never really planned on sickness. And I guess it just never occurred to me that death would eventually 'do us part'. But it did.

We met in college, fell in love, and the week before I graduated with my first BA we were married. We bought a house, raised three boys, added one more, and made our way through the years. October 16, 2016, was the last day of our old life.

Our New Life

Early Monday morning, October 17, 2016, we made our way to the outpatient surgical center for Robb's colonoscopy. Sure, he had been having a little trouble now and then, but the doctor believed he probably had some hemorrhoids or maybe some diverticulosis. The scope was completed, and we were waiting in the little curtained cubicle hoping the doc would come in soon so we could get the discharge paperwork and go grab something to eat. Finally, the doctor came in and said they had found something. *What kind of something?* A mass. *What do you think it is?* Cancer.

....gasp.....suddenly the air left the room....

I felt the kick to the stomach and had to steady myself so as not to fall backwards. I instinctively stepped closer to Robb and took his hand. I don't know who was squeezing harder, Robb or me, but I thought our hands would break. The doctor explained what he found and sent us for blood work and scans. Yes, he sent *us*. Sure, Robb was the one with cancer, but let's face it, we were going to fight this together.

And so the story began.

How To Tell The Children

Tell the kids - how were we going to tell the kids? How do you tell your children that their father has cancer? *So guys, turns out dad has cancer.* How do you stay positive and be there for them when inside you are falling apart? I don't know the answer because I barely remember what I said or how I said it. I cried. I couldn't help it. I could barely get the words out. But I held it together and said what needed to be said and nothing more. I told them we would be seeking out the best doctors and we would fight this. I said that God is bigger than cancer – pray for their father.

They were just like their parents. No overreacting. Asked a few questions and maintained control of their emotions. I'm sure they had their breakdowns, but they only wanted to be supportive of us. Our poor kids. Dealing with such a blow in their 20's. I'm sure they were floored and wondered what it all meant. Well, Matthew and Andrew were. RJ asked medical questions. (RJ is a physician.) He put on his medical hat and approached it like he would approach one of his patients. Yep, just like his mamma.

Tell our families and friends. Call the pastors. Learn how to say the 'C' word without choking. Exist minute by minute, never really fully believing it was real. Pray. Beg God to heal Robb. Beg God not to leave me alone. I hate being alone. I could not imagine life without Robb. This couldn't be happening! Pray harder. Beg more. Remember to exhale.

OK God, Now What Do We Do?

We have always been strong believers and we trusted that God would get us through this. We trusted in His healing. We clung to God's word and the promises of healing and comfort. We told everyone we trusted in God's healing power and asked for prayers for healing. We knew this would be a test of our faith. We had no idea just how much of a test it would be.

Moses said to the people, "Do not fear, for God has come to test you, that the fear of him may be before you, that you may not sin"
Exodus 20:20

Over the next couple days there were scans and more scans. Each result was more cancer. Each result meant more prayer. Always prayer. *("pray without ceasing" 1 Thessalonians 5:17)* God can heal Robb. I know He *can*. I just prayed so hard that He *would* heal Robb – in this life. He had rectal cancer metastatic to his liver and lungs. I don't know how I got through each doctor's visit without crying. I put on my medical caregiver hat and went to work. And prayed. That's all I could do. Robb was scared and overwhelmed (go figure). Well, terrified, and confused, and worried, and anxious, and ….. well, you get it. Me too, but I didn't have time to let my emotions take over. I had to simply press down the fear, press down the anger (I was so angry with God), press down the 'what if's', and just get to work helping find the right doctors and the right treatment. As if anything I did would actually make a difference. I believed that it was my job to find the right doctors. I believed it was my duty to find the right treatments. I failed to see the truth that only God would provide access to whatever doctors and treatments he (God) wanted for Robb. I had no power over this situation apart from prayer. Sure, I prayed, but I didn't fully trust that God had it all under control. I had to do my part to help. I wasn't so much consulting God on what we should do to help him as much as I was telling God what I wanted him to do to help us. Huge mistake.

Many are the plans in the minds of a man, but it is the purpose of the Lord that will stand.
Proverbs 19:21

Who has spoken and it came to pass, unless the Lord has commanded it?
Lamentations 3:37

Our God is in the heavens; he does all that he pleases.
Psalm 115:3

O Lord of hosts, God of Israel, enthroned above the cherubim, you are the God, you alone,
Isaiah 37:16

The Lord of hosts has sworn: "As I have planned, so shall it be, and as I have purposed, so shall it stand"
Isaiah 14:24

We interviewed doctors at various cancer centers to find the one with whom we felt most comfortable. November 3, 2016, was the last day Robb worked. He had been a schoolteacher for 32 years. He hadn't planned on retiring so soon. He was only 55. But there was no way he was going to be able to safely teach while going through chemotherapy. Robb was devastated. *He loved teaching! Why God? Why are you taking this away from him?! Please please please just heal him. I know you can!*

We failed to seek God's guidance. We should not have been asking 'why', we should have been asking 'how'. How do we proceed? How do we get through this? How will you use us in this?

We were naming and claiming a healing. We were praying. Our families and friends were praying. Our coworkers and neighbors and anyone who we talked to was praying. We were hanging onto scripture that promised healing. We trusted God would heal Robb. We told Him so, and we waited.......

Is anyone among you sick? Let him call for the elders of the church, and let them pray over him, anointing him
James 5:14
So we had Robb anointed with oil by the pastors and elders.

And the prayer of faith will save the one who is sick, and the Lord will raise him up
James 5:15
We were all praying.

O Lord my God, I cried to you for help, and you have healed me
Psalm 30:2
We certainly were crying for help!

Heal me, O Lord, and I shall be healed; save me, and I shall be saved, for you are my praise
Jeremiah 17:14

One good thing about living in Moorestown, NJ is that we had a ton of doctor contacts. Robb had coached their kids, or I had been in Home and School with them. I started calling and texting every doctor we knew asking for recommendations for oncologists. Jeff Leavy (cardiologist) and Dean Andrew (vascular surgeon) were the most helpful. Jeff had directed us to the gastroenterologist who had done the colonoscopy (and helped us get an appointment sooner rather than later), and Dean Andrew put us in touch with the oncologist that we ended up using for treatment. Both of them offered help and support along the way. Dean installed Robb's port for chemo and continued to help us navigate the very frightening process. I cannot thank them enough for their kindness and caring. Both awesome docs in their fields and both were willing to go out of their way to help us. Jeff and Dean – if you are reading this, thank you and I love you!

I had to hold it all together and do the only thing I believed I could do - take control of the test results, making the doctor's appointments, finding good doctors, getting second, third, and fourth opinions, arranging for records to be sent, keeping a binder of all test results, and keep track of all the medications. It was as if I was willing his healing to occur. Like I had some control over it. WRONG! My prayers had become a constant chant in my head that ran like an old eight track. As soon as it ended, it rewound and started all over again. I was telling God what I wanted – what I expected. *Heal my Robb. Take away his cancer. Show us what to do. Heal my Robb. Take away his cancer. Show us what to do....* I didn't surrender the situation to God. I wanted to control it. I did everything I knew how to do to affect a positive change and help heal Robb. I put my trust in the medical doctors and my organizational skills. God was just the wing-man. I didn't fully realize that's how I was treating the situation until much later.

I'm kind of an organization expert. I made information sheets to use at all the doctor's appointments. This helped us to not have to write the entire history, medications, doctors, etc. on every form for every doctor. We simply wrote "see attached" and then attached the information sheets. All contacts were stored in my phone and added to a spreadsheet (easily sorted of course).

We were told that with his diagnosis of stage 4 rectal cancer, statistically he had about a 5% chance of surviving 30 months. .....*gasp*..... The doctor said the first chemotherapy would determine if we could stop the spread or at least slow it to give him more time. .....*time*..... The chart read 'terminal' but I didn't tell Robb. That's the day I started to grieve. I grieved the loss of what we had – a normal life. And although I prayed for God's healing in this life (and believed God *could* heal Robb), I didn't actually believe it was going to happen. Somehow I knew it wasn't in the cards and I started to grieve his loss even though he was still very much alive, for now.......so I prayed harder. And, let's face it, I took more responsibility to find the right treatments! As if the medical doctors and I could somehow outperform God. AS IF!

November 9, 2016, he started chemotherapy at MD Anderson at Cooper in Camden, NJ. Robb was having some trouble with constipation – turns out it's because his tumor was growing and partially obstructing his bowel. Seriously! I had no idea someone could have such relatively insignificant symptoms and have a tumor the size of a baseball in their colon!

PSA: Get screened! Get tested! Have the colonoscopy at age 50 as recommended. Have yearly mammograms and pap smears. Do what you can to help catch cancer early and improve your chances of long term survival.

They hoped the chemo would kick the cancer to the curb. Sadly, it only kicked Robb. He had six sessions of one kind of chemo that made him really sick – terrible stomach aches and headaches, body aches, flu-like symptoms, gave him bad neuropathy – he couldn't touch anything cooler than body temperature without feeling like he was being stabbed in the fingertips, he lost most of his hair on his body, and had horrible fatigue, but the tumors grew and his constipation got worse.

O God in heaven, please please please heal my husband! Then I would press down the fear (holy moly was I scared), press down the anger (boy oh boy was I angry), and just work harder to find treatment that worked and help with his side effects.

God tried to speak to me through his word, but I guess I wasn't quite ready to really listen. I read my Bible and looked for encouragement and hope. I longed for hope.

Do not be anxious about anything, but in everything by prayer and supplication with thanksgiving let your requests be made known to God
Philippians 4:6

Well, I was anxious. But I was making my requests (ok, more like demands) known to God. But things didn't get any better. They got worse.

The Back Story

Robb was in a bad accident in 2003 while coaching lacrosse. He broke his neck, had cervical spinal fusion, and had spinal cord damage. Fun times. In 2009 he was diagnosed with type 1 diabetes. Yep. In his 40's. It's not Murphy's Law, clearly, it's Murray's Law. He was thrilled. Do you believe me? No? Really? Well, what would you believe?

Back To The Story.....

The chemo affected his diabetes. It was a nightmare. Thankfully Dr. Vincent Savarese (endocrinologist of the year in my opinion) and Judith Singley (diabetic educator extraordinaire) helped us navigate the crazy blood sugar swings. The oncologist Dr. Alexandre Hageboutros wanted to get him through six sessions so then (supposedly) it would hold the cancer back while he had radiation of the rectal tumor. The plan was to irradiate it, let it heal a bit, then resect the bowel to remove the tumor and bad bowel tissue. That was the doctor's plan. That was our plan.

That was the plan, but as we came to find out, God had other plans.

*"For my thoughts are not your thoughts, neither are your ways my ways,"
declares the Lord. "For as the heavens are higher than the earth, so are
my ways higher than your ways and my thoughts than your thoughts."*
Isaiah 55:8-9

God Has His Own Plans

Three days before he was scheduled to start radiation, he experienced
a complete bowel obstruction and was rushed to the hospital for
emergency surgery. *Seriously? This can't be happening!* That's the
first thing that came to mind when Dr. Hageboutros told us to go
straight to the hospital. The second thing was *please God heal my
Robb!* I was getting really good at telling God what I wanted Him
to do and when I wanted Him to do it. Now, God just needed to
come through. I was treating God like a pez dispenser for my prayer
requests (well more like prayer demands than actual requests). I kept
asking for my plan – not His plan. Mistake....... There I was again,
press down the fear, press down the anger.

Rush to the hospital, call the kids, text the pastors, admitted to
the hospital, put in a room and quickly prepped for surgery. No
time to really think about it. No time to lose it. Just keep doing,
answering questions, respond to texts, and pray. That day, sitting
in the hospital room with Robb, I prayed harder than I think I had
ever prayed. It wasn't as though I was actually forming words in my
head. It was more like I had a constant exchange of thoughts with
God. Somehow, I had accessed a part of my brain that could actually
commune with God while I was going about the business of helping
everyone get Robb ready for surgery. I didn't fully understand it at
the time, but that was the first time during this whole process that I
was actually in touch with the Holy Spirit that indwells all believers.
It was the first time this had happened to me as an adult, but it was

not the last. I remember this same feeling when I was a small child. But that's another story. Back to this one.

Just as they were coming to get Robb to take him down to the OR for surgery, Pastor HeyYoung Horton arrived. I didn't know she was coming, but clearly she had dropped everything and rushed to the hospital when she got my text. I was so thankful she was there. And so was Robb. She walked down with us to the area just outside the OR where they put in an IV and the anesthesiologist and surgeon spoke with us. They assured us all would be fine.

I told them all that we had so many people praying for Robb and for the surgical team. I felt so small and insignificant as I said the words. Almost like the words were being swallowed up by the enormity of the situation. I didn't 'feel' the power of Christ that I was telling the surgical team we were praying for. Instead, I felt the earth shift beneath me, and I knew for sure that nothing was going to be the same again. I knew as surely as I am sitting here today, I knew that our entire world would never be the same again. We were never going back to our old life. We might not even have much life together left. My heart was pounding, my breathing was quick and shallow, I could feel the adrenaline pumping, I started to shake, and I almost started to panic. Almost. *Please God, please!* That's all I could muster. My mind raced. I couldn't find the words. I turned to that inward place again and simply held out my arms like a child who wants to be picked up by a parent. Then my heart rate slowed, my breathing was normal, and the shaking stopped. God had wrapped His arms around me and assured me that He was here with us no matter what we faced. I held Robb's hand and prayed that God would assure Robb the way he had done for me.

Robb was shaken by the whole situation, and he was visibly annoyed. He said, "This wasn't the plan. This isn't how it's supposed to go!" Pastor HeyYoung very calmly said, "Step out of the boat."

Immediately another wave of calm came over me. A calm I had not felt before. Robb looked at her, clearly not understanding what she meant. She said, "Step out of the boat and keep your eyes on Jesus." She continued, "God must have another plan for you. It's not your plan that matters, its God's. Trust in Him."

He said, "Come." So Peter got out of the boat and walked on the water and came to Jesus. But when he saw the wind, he was afraid, and beginning to sink he cried out, "Lord, save me." Jesus immediately reached out his hand and took hold of him, saying to him, "O you of little faith, why did you doubt?" And when they got into the boat, the wind ceased. And those in the boat worshipped him, saying, "Truly you are the Son of God." Matthew 14:29-33

Then she prayed with us. Robb wasn't so willing to step out of the boat. Looks like God was going to turn the boat over in order to get Robb out of the boat! Lesson – don't think about not trusting His plan. Just don't. We already tried that and it didn't work out well. 'Nough said.

The nurse appeared next to the bed and ushered Robb into emergency surgery to bypass the tumor and affected colon. They performed a colostomy. But they did not remove the tumor. *WHY? WHY DID THEY NOT TAKE OUT THE CANCER WHILE THEY WERE IN THERE?!!!!*

Robb came to in the recovery area. He was angry, in pain, angry, felt so wiped out, and he was angry. Did I mention he was angry? *This wasn't our plan! Why are you doing this God?!*

Note: God was with us every step of the way. I was angry and taking it out on God because we were going through this. God never promised perfect days of cupcakes, unicorns, and rainbows. He promised to walk with us and use every situation for His good.

"I have said these things to you, that in me you may have peace. In the world you will have tribulation. But take heart; I have overcome the world."
John 16:33

Angry

Robb was angry. I had to finally admit, I was angry too. *Why wasn't God healing my husband like I asked? We are good Christians with a strong faith. Surely God would heal Robb. Why wasn't He making the tumors shrink? I know God has the power to do it, so why wasn't He? Why hasn't He?* Then that anger had to be pushed aside because I had work to do. I didn't have time to be angry. I had to simply press down the anger, press down the fear, and I had to dive in and do everything in my power to get Robb the best care and find a way to heal him. *C'mon God, show me what to do.* As if I could somehow cause the healing by finding the right doctors, the right chemo, the right foods, the right whatever. As if.... Clearly I still had not learned my lesson.

He was admitted to the hospital of course, but didn't get a room for 46 hours! Yes, he was in the little tiny recovery cubical for 46 hours. Can you imagine the fun? I was the only visitor because there was just no room for anyone else. They didn't get him out of bed – there wasn't anywhere to do that. I had asked every nurse if they had him on the list for a room. Every one of them assured me he was. Finally, on day two, I found the head nurse and explained what was going on. She discovered that he was not on a list to get a room and had never been on a list for a room. I was furious. She said she would put him on the list. I told her with the kindest sweetest smile I could muster that she better make some calls and he better be the next one to get a room, not wait in line – he had already waited two days! Then I suggested that she tell her nurses to take the initiative to check the list when a patient has been waiting longer than their required three hours in recovery. I was really angry. I was ready to explode angry! I remembered when Jesus was angry and made a whip to drive out the money changers in the temple. I was feeling like that. Good thing there was nothing handy with which to fashion a whip. Again – no time for that. Press down the anger and get to work taking care of Robb. (Just a little sidenote: pressing down the anger over and over is not really the best idea. It finds a way of getting loose when you least expect it.)

Once he was finally in a room, he was in the hospital a couple days. His diabetes is always part of the equation and we had lots of fun arguing with the medical staff about where his blood sugar should be and how we were very capable of managing with his pump. Well, when I say 'we' I mean, me and Judith Singley. She is the most amazing soul. I could text or call her any time and she would drop everything and help us. If it weren't for her, Robb would have been back on the hospital drip (not as efficient as a pump) and inpatient for many additional days. Thank you Judith – we love you! God used her to help Robb. God was constantly working, multitasking to make everything fall into place as HE planned. I wasn't ready to surrender to his plan yet......

But I digress. Back to Robb in the hospital post colostomy. The staff was over-worked and often not able to tend to his ostomy bag as often as was needed and I did some things that I never imagined when I said "I do", but what I was willing to do anything to help my husband. I had to take over his ostomy care. He couldn't get the hang of it. Or was it more that he just felt too overwhelmed by it? Likely the latter. He was surviving one minute at a time just like me, but he was the one facing death, and a slow painful one at that. My heart broke for him. All the time.

During all this time (his diagnosis, treatments, surgery) almost no one came to visit. Very few called. Some texted. Many commented on the social media posts. That is virtually the only support Robb got (other than from me and our kids). I was part of a prayer group on messenger. I had my cousin Pamela Shannon and my friend Lynn Saia that I could count on day or night. They were always just a text or call away. Both amazing godly women who helped me through the most difficult time in my life. God put them in my life for exactly that purpose and I am so grateful. That was the only real support I got. Yes, Robb was the one experiencing all the treatments, side effects, pain, etc., but I was going through too! I was terrified, and angry, and exhausted, and couldn't function some days but still had to in order to take care of him. FYI if you know someone who is a caregiver to a very ill person, please support them also. Sometimes they have a smile on their face when really they are dying inside.

No, He's Not Radioactive

But I digress. Again. Tangential thoughts often plague me.

Back to February 2017 and the emergency colostomy. After two short weeks of recovery, Robb began chemotherapy with radiation. Five days a week for twenty eight sessions (about six weeks). Every day I drove him to MD Anderson at Cooper in Camden, NJ. On Monday's we would first go wait at infusion, get hooked up to a chemo bag that he had to wear all week constantly being infused. After that he would head down to radiation where he waited for his turn, he changed his clothes, waited for his turn, received about fifteen minutes of radiation, changed back into his clothes, and I drove us home. Every Friday, we would end by going up to infusion and waiting to be de-accessed (disconnected so at least he had a weekend without that bag attached to him). Every day. Rain, snow, sleet, all of it. From February 15 through March 29, 2017. I would bring my crochet hooks and yarn and would pray and make hats for the infusion unit while I waited. I said lots of prayers and made a lot of hats….. I found comfort in using my time to talk to God and help others who were suffering. I attached Bible verse cards to each hat and prayed that the Holy Spirit would work miracles in the life of the person to whom the hat was given.

The position (for radiation) on the hard table would press on his port (left clavicle). He said it was rather painful. We couldn't have that! So I fashioned a little pillow with a hole in it that fit around the port and cushioned it on the table. He said it was much better. The nurses liked it so much that I made them a whole bag full. Other patients in the waiting room saw them and wanted them too. A small thing but it really makes a difference when you already feel so yucky and hurt so much. I asked God to show me what I can do to help people. He showed me every day. This was a change for me. I didn't tell God what to do, I didn't tell God what I was doing and how He could help Me; instead, I asked God to show me what He wanted Me to do to help others. My attitude began to shift……

The effects of the radiation were grueling. The worst was the fatigue. He described it as being the most tired he had ever been. That he didn't even have the energy to lift his arms some days. The bag got in the way of sleeping so he would try to sleep on the sofa or in the recliner. Neither provided very good sleep. The chemo gave him constipation (great – just what he needed) so he had to take lots and lots of medications to help alleviate the problem. We were never sure how much was too much (hey, when you can't go and you're in pain, you are willing to try whatever it takes to resolve the problem). Sometimes, the medications worked a little too well and….. Oh joy. With an ostomy bag that's less fun than one would think.

Someone asked if they could be around him since he was 'radioactive'. *Really? Did they really believe that? Seriously, he's not radioactive.* With my nicest sweetest smile I explained what radiation is. Sigh….. But

I noticed a difference in how I prayed and how I approached Robb's care. I was (slowly) shifting control back to God (not that I was ever in control – I only thought I was).

Our lives turned into just getting Robb to and from his appointments and managing his side effects. No social life. No sex life. No fun. Our friends were off on vacations, cruises, going out to dinner, going to concerts. We were going to the hospital and back home. It would have really torn us apart if it weren't for God holding us together. I would post updates and prayer requests on *Robb Murray's Wild Ride*. I felt a sense of connection with the people reading the updates. Robb loved seeing who commented or who reacted to the posts. It really helped him. I did get a little annoyed that very few people actually texted or messaged us. Almost no one called. I guess people didn't want to bother us knowing just how badly Robb was feeling. All the time. It was a very difficult time. We held onto each other and we held onto God for dear life. That eight track chant kept playing in my head.

We were holding onto God's word:
But they who wait for the Lord shall renew their strength; they shall mount up with wings like eagles; they shall run and not be weary; they shall walk and not faint
Isaiah 40:31

Ask, and it will be given to you; seek, and you will find; knock, and it will be opened to you
Matthew 7:7

And I tell you, ask, and it will be given to you; seek, and you will find; knock, and it will be opened to you
Luke 11:9

We certainly were asking! We were seeking! We were waiting for the time when Robb would mount up with wings like eagles and run.

So, God, You're Still Not Listening?

He finished chemo/radiation on March 29, 2017, and two weeks later had more scans. We begged God for positive results – let the cancer have shrunk. The results showed that the liver tumors had basically gone crazy. They had multiplied and grown. Well, this was really bad news. Originally, we were told that after the chemo/radiation we would decide if Robb was having the ostomy reversed first or the cancer in the liver removed. They had planned to simply remove the one part of the liver that was originally affected by cancer. The scans clearly showed that the chemo had not held the cancer at bay and that it was alive and well and making itself at home in my husband. Now the whole liver was affected so that took resection off the table – forever.

I had a quick heart to heart with God right there in the doctor's office.
Me: Really God?! REALLY?
God: Trust me.

That is when I knew for sure there would not be miraculous healing …. *he really wouldn't beat this. God really isn't going to heal him in this life.* The chemo hadn't worked. In fact, it didn't seem to do anything except make him sick. He had suffered all those horrible side effects for nothing! I almost panicked. Almost. I had that same mental communion with God and a calm came over me. We had more work to do. God wasn't done with Robb yet. Not if I had anything to say about it (like I actually had a say – I clearly wasn't fully listening to God yet….. yet).

Let's Try This Now

April 2017 we went to see the oncologist again. He told us he wanted to try a "more robust" chemotherapy. It was definitely "more robust". He should have just said stronger and the side effects would be worse. Way worse.

And so the next chapter began. Every other week we drove to the hospital, saw the doctor, then went upstairs to infusion. We waited until a chair was available. Once Robb was settled into the comfy reclining chair, TV on, warm blanket over him, I would arrange all the stuff I brought for the long day, plop into the hard plastic chair next to him (the life of the caregiver) and start arranging all our things. His diabetic testing supplies next to him, the medications he would need to manage side effects on the top of my handbag, his drink and lunch or snacks on the table next to him, my crochet hooks and yarn on my lap, his phone placed on the side table next to him, my phone tucked under my thigh because there wasn't anywhere for me to put stuff, and we waited for our favorite nurse Maria Metzler, RN. Of course we loved all the nurses, but we had a very special bond with Maria. She is a strong woman of faith and told us she was praying for Robb. When things didn't go right (like when his blood pressure was way too high to treat, or when they had a problem with the port so they wouldn't treat) she would always stay calm and pray for him. She would try every trick in the book to make things go as smoothly as possible for him. We would always looked forward to hearing about her grandchildren and seeing the creative things her daughter made. God had given us a blessing in the midst of the horror. A very godly woman who cared deeply for her patients – for Robb. She was seeking his guidance and made Robb's care a little less horrible. I am so grateful for her.

The port would be accessed, the premeds would run, and Robb would try to prepare (mentally) for the next bags to be hung – the horrible terrible awful poison that would make him sicker than he's ever been, but that we hoped and prayed was killing the cancer and not him. His stomach would start to hurt. He would get wildly nauseous. His head would pound. His joints would ache. There would be a horrible taste in his mouth. The poison would be infused over five plus hours. The side effects would begin while he was at the infusion center but would increase tenfold when we got home. We developed a routine.

Finish at the chemo unit and he would wait while I got the car warmed up, seat reclined, and meds ready in the center console. Get Robb home and into the house, into jammie bottoms, into his recliner with an ice pack on his head/neck, a heating pad on his stomach, and a light blanket over him. Give him heavy duty pain meds and every stomach cramp, nausea, vomiting, feel better medicine he had along with a bunch of over-the-counter stuff, and pray. Pray that his side effects would subside. Pray that he would feel better. Pray that God would heal my husband. Beg God to heal him (while not really believing that God would). Then post an update on *Robb Murray's Wild Ride* asking everyone to pray for Robb. What a horrible existence for my poor husband. All because he wanted to fight so hard to stay alive for me and our children. He was willing to endure all of that suffering for us. Heartbreaking and humbling.

This was our life. (I had no life apart from taking care of Robb.) Have treatment. Manage side effects. Try to work when Robb was okay enough for me to leave him. Our fun consisted of sitting on the sofa binge watching Netflix. Thank God it's cheap and there's lots of options. We 'visited' faraway lands and saw spectacular historical events. All thanks to the miracle of cinematography. Of course I secretly wished we were actually experiencing all the wonderful places, but we didn't get to go anywhere or do anything. Robb just didn't feel well enough. My heart broke for him. All the time. I still found myself pressing down the fear and anger. I didn't know what else to do with it.

Some Sunshine In Our Rainy Life

May brought a wonderful treat – our son RJ's engagement party. This wasn't just any party. This was THE PARTY! He and his beautiful (then) fiancée Calla Vodoor had about 200 of their closest family and friends be part of their Hindu betrothal ceremony and Celtic Christian Handfasting Ceremony. Of course there was food and dancing. And a lot of fun. We really needed that. We almost didn't make it to the party because Robb was feeling so poorly. But God made a way and we enjoyed the day. I must say, Robb looked especially good in his Murray clan kilt!

Help Was On The Way

By summer of 2017 things were starting to get really difficult for us, both emotionally as well as financially. Even with 'good' insurance, copays, coinsurances, out of pocket costs, non-covered treatments, etc. things were getting to be way more than we could handle. We had already exhausted all of our savings. Many people had been generous and helped us (which was amazing and always came at just the right time – God's hand evident), but expenses were growing.

Many people were asking if they could help us make an online donation page, but we just weren't too excited about the idea. It felt wrong. For us. I had made a webpage with suggestions on how to help. I posted it on the *Robb Murray's Wild Ride* FB page and made the post it public so others could share. Then I just trusted that God would provide. And He did. He always does. [I will include a copy of what was posted later in the book. It can be used as a guide for how you can help other families going through this kind of thing.]

The treatments went on. And on. And on. We were feeling defeated. We just needed a break! We had been talking about how we would go to Scotland once Robb was better. Even if he would just feel enough like traveling and it was safe for him to go for just a week. It was looking like we would never get to go. And we could never afford it anyway. It became one more thing we would only dream about. We had decided that if we couldn't go to Scotland, maybe we could at least go to Boston. Neither of us had ever done the freedom trail, seen the North Church, or seen the historic sites where our founders had once lived and worked. We are huge American history buffs so this would be really cool.

No idea how we would manage it. Physically Robb wasn't up to much at all. Financially there was simply no way. We had a big 30th wedding anniversary trip planned in May 2016, but that had to be cancelled because my mom was dying. We figured we would just be able to the following year instead. But Robb was diagnosed in October 2016. That big anniversary trip was never going to happen….. But we prayed it would and asked God to provide for us.

Dreaming of Scotland

Our (then) daughter-in-law to be Calla decided she wanted to help us get to Scotland. She organized a collection asking all their friends if they would be willing to help us get to Scotland. We had no idea she was doing any of this. One night, she and RJ came to the house. They said they had something they wanted to give us. Calla read what she had circulated to her friends, read about how she wanted to help us, then RJ and Calla gave us a beautiful shadowbox frame with pictures and encouraging messages from many of their friends. It was so sweet. Then they handed us an envelope and said it's enough to get us to Scotland! Robb broke down and cried. So did I! She had also made a 'backup plan for Boston' complete with ideas of places to stay and things to see and do. How amazing. God is so good. Just when we were feeling the most defeated, God put a smile on our face and some hope back in our hearts.

Help Lord Murray The Kilted Celt Kick Cancer to the Curb!

Our sons and my sister Karen Hare Eder had wanted to do a benefit. Karen asked her friends Mark and Shanna Oberg (she had grown up with Shanna) if we could use their new place – Curran's Irish Inn. They worked out all the details and planned an amazing benefit for October 2017. (The owners rebranded Curran's, it's now called 5 West, 5 W Broad St., Palmyra, NJ - shameless plug for them – the owners are wonderful people and the food is delicious). They collected donation items for raffle baskets. They raffled off over 30 baskets! Many worth over $300 each. Many many people attended. People we had not heard from prior to this. It was so comforting to know that so many people were there to support Robb. He really needed it. We all did. We were so thankful that he was feeling well enough to attend – he even stayed for the entire night! They raised enough money to pay for the very expensive FoundationOne genetic testing that is not covered by insurance. What a blessing. God provides.

Boston or Bust!

Since we were living one day to the next with how Robb was feeling, we decided, quite last minute, that we really wanted to go away as soon as Robb was feeling up to it. We didn't know what was coming next or how it would make Robb feel. It was now or never. Inside of three days, with the help of Calla and her cousin (who lives in Boston), we planned a getaway. Calla was going to help us book a hotel. I told her we would drive so that no matter how Robb was feeling we could just leave if needed. I asked her to look for a Residence Inn or some kind of place that had a separate sitting area (knowing that he often feels horrible so we might be sitting in a hotel room watching TV). RJ called me to tell me they booked a hotel and he would send us the confirmation. He said it's a suite and that he and Calla had paid for it as a Christmas gift. *WHAT?!!!! That's amazing!!!*

I packed our bags (lots of them – we had to be prepared for anything that might happen while we were there) and we were off! I had to do all the driving which is never easy for me. But it got us where we wanted to be so I was willing do it. We planned to stop half way up and half way back to do a little sightseeing and stretch our legs. We arrived at the hotel. Went up to our room. There was our wedding picture, a bottle of wine, chocolates, and two bathrobes. *How sweet!* RJ and Calla had arranged it with the hotel manager. Of course I cried. The next couple days we planned our outings carefully to allow for Robb to have plenty of time to get himself together in the morning, rest in the car on our way to and from each location, eat at regular intervals (remember he is a diabetic), and be back to the hotel early enough for him to vegetate on the sofa and watch TV.

It was a wonderful vacation even though it wasn't the dream vacation we had hoped for. Robb still had bad days and we had to do less than we had planned. At least we did get to see the North Church and walk a little bit of the Freedom Trail. I wish it had been a romantic second honeymoon, but that just wasn't in the cards. So we settled for seeing something new and enjoying the history. We would often say, "when Robb does get better, we are going to plan one amazing trip to Scotland! I KNOW our God can heal Robb." We were (not so) patiently waiting on the Lord. I would say those things, but knew in my heart Robb's healing would not come in this life – only in the next. So I pressed down the fear. Pressed down the anger. And carried on.

I still begged God to heal Robb. I knew God *could* heal Robb and I just could not understand why he wasn't. We prayed. Our families prayed. Our friends prayed. Our church families prayed. And we waited....... I waited....... I impatiently waited for God all the time secretly knowing that I was going to end up alone – that healing would not come in this life – only in the next......

Home For The Holidays (and every other day)

The days dragged on and the treatments continued. Thanksgiving, Christmas, and New Year were less fanfare than previous years. We couldn't have anyone in the house who was sick. Family members were all sick for Thanksgiving and Christmas. I cooked and provided take-out for the sick family members. We had about half a dozen of us for Thanksgiving dinner and only four of us for Christmas dinner. New Year's Eve for us was go to bed early and pray we could actually sleep. No fun-filled parties or celebrations. What we celebrated was another year together. That's what mattered. We prayed for healing in the next year, less side effects, less pain, more fun, and getting back to living again. We knew God *could* do it, we just prayed that He *would*.

Alternative Medicine

We put the word out that we were looking for any and all treatment options – even alternative treatments. In January 2018, Judith Singley called to tell us about a doctor/Qigong Master whom she had met. She was optimistic that he may be able to help Robb. He was an M.D., trained in China, as well as a Qigong Master. He had moved to the USA and began practicing in California years ago.

I purchased his book and started reading. I strongly believe that there is energy (from God) that we cannot see that God and his angels are at work in this world that we cannot see, but that affect us daily. What I read was intriguing. I had argued one time that much of the alternative medicine dealing with energy is simply science that had not yet been proven. Imagine if we spoke to someone in the 1700's and talked about germs. They would think we were conjuring demons! They had not yet discovered the microorganisms we know to cause illness and disease. It is the same today. What we don't yet understand doesn't have to be voodoo or magic. Perhaps it's simply science that we don't yet understand. They were the same thoughts attributed to the doctor's mother when he was a child. I kept reading.

I had some very serious concerns. Where does he claim he gets these powers? He says he simply harnesses the energy of the universe. Hmmmmmm.......okay and where does the universe get its power?

There is power from God, and power from evil. I contacted Pastor HeyYoung and asked her opinion. I poured out all my concerns. She was born and raised in Korea, but is a trained Christian pastor, so she was able to understand both worlds – the alternative practice of Qigong as well as the Christian perspective. She said, "All good things come from God. All healing comes from God. I say try it!" So we did.

[Note: I would not recommend doing this. It became clear that this was NOT from God and we should have run from it, not toward it. But we were scared and grasping at straws and the pastor said it was okay. I only include the next parts because they show just how desperate people can become when faced with death. Even good Christians can be duped by forces not from God. And, God has a sense of humor and showed me how to laugh in spite of our choices.]

I contacted the doctor and scheduled appointments for both of us to see him at his office in City of Industry, California. Big step for me. That meant booking flights (we don't fly anywhere). Booking a hotel (we don't go anywhere). Renting a car (I like my car). Figuring out all the details of the trip and trying to also factor in some sightseeing. Well, if we are going all the way to CA, I want to see some stuff while we are there! My three biggies – put my feet in the Pacific Ocean, visit the tar pits, and see the Hollywood sign. I know, how touristy. Whatever. I could play the tourist!

Fortunately, once I posted that we needed help finding a hotel and flights, our friends Myrrh and Joe Winston contacted us and said they are only about twenty minutes from City of Industry and we could stay with them. YAY!!!! I miss them sooooooo much since they moved from Moorestown, NJ. It would be so much fun to visit with them. Also, Myrrh is a nurse so any issue we had while we were there, she could certainly help us.

LAX - The Land Of Lunacy

We arrived in CA, found our way to car rental place (don't know how, but we did), got the bags loaded and found our way out of LAX. I really dislike LAX. I mean, 'dislike' is not a strong enough word. We were starving, looked in GoogleMaps for restaurants, but the GPS kept trying to take us to Compton. I wasn't really interested in eating lunch in Compton. So we kept driving. I was exhausted, had a splitting headache, was famished, and felt like maybe we had made a mistake going to CA. Just when I thought I had reached the end of my rope, we found a place to eat in a nice plaza far outside of Compton. Whew. Thank you God! We ate and got back on the road. Only about a half hour to our friend's house in Yorba Linda.

We picked up groceries on the way. Drove to their house. Had lots of hugs. And moved into vacation mode. Drinks were poured. Their neighbor met us at the dock out back, and everyone went for a lovely ride on the lake. The weather was warm, the sun was shining, and watching the ducks and hummingbirds was a welcomed activity after the nightmare that was our travel. We had a wonderful time catching up. It had been years since we last saw them.

Doctor / Qigong Grandmaster - Interesting Combination

Dr. Liu's office was only about a fifteen-minute drive from Myrrh and Joe's house. Myrrh drove (thank God – our rental car looked like the scene of a homicide - literally). As we pulled up to the office building, we saw an older Asian man sitting on the garden wall smoking a cigarette. He was wearing what appeared to be a Chinese suit (with the arms and pant bottoms cuffed). I recognized him from the cover of his book. However, the photo on the book was obviously from decades past. As we were gathering our things, he put out the cigarette and went inside.

We headed into the building, up to his office (which was rather unassuming, small, and quite cluttered – a surprise considering just how well-known this guy was supposed to be), and there he was – the guy we had just seen outside. NO WAY! An M.D. and Qigong Master and he smokes? In my head I was cracking up. We turned in our paperwork and talked with the very sweet assistant/translator/ exercise instructor/billing person/girl Friday. No sooner had we done this, and Dr. Liu / Master Hong was whisking me back to his office to do my evaluation. I was skeptical. Very skeptical. That's my nature. Question everything. I wasn't impressed with the evaluation, but I was still willing to 'play along'.

I Paid An Old Chinese Guy To Spank Me

We went into another room – a small treatment room. He asked me to face the wall and close my eyes. He said he was going to examine me. Although I could not see what he was doing, I could clearly feel that one hand was hovering over the top of my head and the other was moving slowly down my back (but never actually touching me). I felt a very strange sensation – a rush of what I can only describe as energy. I felt the warmth and the waves of energy. I had already prayed that God would protect us from anything not of God. Now I began praying that God would protect my body, my thoughts, and my mind, from the forces of evil. I don't know where this guy gets his 'powers' and I wanted to be absolutely sure it didn't hurt me. That lasted only a minute or two. I kept remembering Matthew 12:30 and Luke 11:23: Whoever is not with me is against me, and whoever does not gather with me scatters. He didn't acknowledge God as his source of energy; therefore, I had to assume he was not 'with God', so I prayed a hedge of protection around myself. I should have left right then. But I didn't......

Then he instructed me to sit on a small stool facing a low treatment table much like a physical therapy table. He then told me to pull up my shirt and hike down my pants exposing my back and top of my pants line. I complied. He began to spank me with the back of his hand. No lie. He was spanking me! I was shocked and quite annoyed! It didn't hurt. Not at first. It just felt like he was slapping me, but not hard. He asked if it hurt. No. He kept it up. Suddenly, I had searing pain where he was slapping me. I started to breathe heavily and broke out in a sweat. What in the world was he doing? He really had not changed anything he was doing so I couldn't understand why this suddenly hurt so badly. I prayed and prayed. I should have told him to stop and left. But I didn't.....

He stopped, and asked to use my phone camera to take a picture of my back so I could see what he had done. As I was getting out my phone and opening the camera, I was yelling for Robb and Myrrh to come in. They both saw what the doctor showed me in the picture he took. Right where it hurt, there was a small black spot and a lump. He said I had a herniated disc and he was "drawing out the bad energy to heal it". I do have a herniated disc. It does bother me. I had not told him this. I asked Myrrh to look at the spot. She is a nurse. I trusted that she would have a logical explanation. I was convinced it was only a swollen blood vessel (after all, he had just been spanking me). Nope. Not a swollen blood vessel. She had no idea what it was. Then he began to spank me again. Seriously? What?! Suddenly the pain stopped and one smack later he stopped even though I had not told him the pain stopped. The lump had grown – seeming to have come to the surface. He said it was the bad energy.

I was permitted to pull down my shirt and pull up my pants. Then he asked to tie my hair up and started the same process on my neck.

What?! Same thing as with my low back. Same annoyance, then pain, then stopped. More bad energy. Wow.

I don't know why I didn't tell him to stop and just leave. I don't know why I knew this was not of God and still stayed. I regret that decision.

He finished and sent me off to learn exercises to help center my Qi while he took Robb into his office. I wanted to go with him but couldn't. After a few minutes, I saw Robb was in the treatment room. I told the assistant I had to go watch my husband's treatment. I got to the room as the doctor had one hand over his head and the other near his back. He was grabbing the air and 'throwing' it away. He explained he was drawing out the bad energy and getting rid of it. What was interesting was that I saw some type of energy being transferred between the doctor's hand and Robb's head. Almost like the heat waves you see coming off a very hot roadway. I was astounded. I began to pray a hedge of protection around Robb. Not sure where in the universe his powers came from (although I had my suspicions), I was going to be sure to ask God to protect Robb from any unwanted demonic influence.

He instructed Robb to sit on the same stool. He asked him to pull up his shirt and hike down his pants. Then he spanked my husband. Yep. We paid an old Chinese man to spank us. What in the world were going to tell people about what his treatments were?!

We finished, paid (a lot of money), and drove back to Myrrh and Joe's. The whole way back we talked about what had happened, what we had seen, what we had felt. We discussed the strange diet the doctor had recommended and wondered how we would ever stick to it! Duck – no chicken or turkey. Black rice. Black walnuts. Mushrooms. Nagaimo (ya, no clue, I had to Google that one) – turns out it's a Chinese yam. I'm sure I can find that in ShopRite, right? The diet would have to wait until we got home.

As we were driving (in traffic) it occurred to me that my back wasn't hurting like it had been. Surely a coincidence. Robb and Myrrh said they had not seen the strange heat waves that I had seen. Robb had not felt the pulsing sensation that I had felt. They said I saw and felt it because "you're a conjure-woman". (I use herbs, oils, natural medicine, and my family calls me a conjure-woman. Ya, they make fun of me but they ask me to make them concoctions for everything from acne, menstrual cramps, or sinus pain, to allergies, headaches, and sleep problems.) Conjure-woman or not, I know what I saw and felt. I had a lot to pray about. And a lot of rebuking of evil to do.

How Long Can This Go On?

Back to New Jersey and back to treatments as usual. He had more bad days than good. This went on for one year. Exactly 12 months, 24 cycles. Each scan would show a little growth. How many times can you have a little and a little and a little before you finally realize that a bunch of little's equals a lot?

Robb's cancer marker in his blood had started out at 13 when he was diagnosed in October 2016. In April 2017 it was 42. In April 2018 it was 364. It was time to look for clinical trials, try oral chemo, and investigate radioembolization of the liver, anything that might be able to stop this nasty beast. More doctors. No systemic therapy – he had to be off of chemo in order to prepare for experimental medicine. He had to be off of all treatment for six weeks before he could do a clinical trial. Kind of scary. Okay, more than kind of scary. *What is the cancer doing? Is it going to go crazy again? Please God heal my Robb!* Press down the fear. Press down the frustration. Press down the anger. Just get to work and ignore the feelings boiling inside.

That wasn't my best decision….. Turns out when you ignore your feelings of anger, fear, and frustration, they have a way of rearing their ugly heads at times and places you never intended. Sometimes with crazy emotional outbursts, and sometimes as physical illnesses. Ya, not my best decision…..

Trials

I put out a request on FB and texted everyone I could think of. I asked if anyone knows anyone who works at any hospitals with cancer treatment centers. I wanted to get as many inside contacts as possible. Once I had inside contacts, I would ask them for their contacts to the cancer treatment area of their hospital. This proved exhaustingly time consuming but amazingly helpful. I was amazed at just how incredibly helpful people wanted to be. It was encouraging.

I went on the government site for clinical trials and researched every trial for which he might be eligible. Reading every trial (often 20+ pages long) and trying to determine if Robb met the exclusion and inclusion criteria for participation. Once I found one that might be good and for which he might qualify, I would bring a printed copy with me to the oncologist. I read over 180 trials in one week. I brought a stack of fifteen printed trials to the oncologist. Only two were actually ones with merit so I contacted those trial directors. One trial was at Columbia. I managed to get an inside contact there who helped me work my way up the chain to the doctor who was overseeing the trial. We got an appointment. YAY! We had hope! Thank you Mohan Vodoor!!!!

We went to UPenn and Columbia (at NYU) to talk about clinical trials. UPenn said he was eligible and even had us sign the consent forms. *YAY!!!!* Then they called two days later to say the sponsor rejected him. *Huge letdown.* Columbia said he was eligible *(YAY!)*

but the trial had been placed on voluntary hold the day before *(ugh)*. Huger letdown (yes, that's a word, huger – more huge than). They suggested we seek radioembolization of the liver while we wait for the trial to reopen.

I had another heart to heart with God.

Me: Hey God - It wasn't supposed to be like this! We were supposed to get into the Columbia trial and Robb was supposed to be healed! Why was this not working the way we wanted?!

God: Hey Conni – did you forget that I'm in charge and your plan isn't what matters? Do you trust me?

Me: Well, yes, but, (He cut me off mid word)

God: No But – Do you trust me?

Me: Yes.

God: Then pull yourself together and stop questioning – just trust.

So, as it turns out, we found out a few weeks later that the reason the trial was placed on hold was because it worked a little too well.... in that, the tumors expanded prior to dissipating; however, a tumor that's in an airway may stop airflow. Robb had tumors in his lungs. We also found out that anyone with preexisting cardiac issues had severe cardiac failure......we also found out later that Robb had a silent cardiac issue and the trial would have killed him. So, when God closed that door, I should not have been whining and complaining, I should have been thanking him and asking what he wanted us to do.

Y90 – The Fun Stops Here

We got an appointment to see Dr. Sabina Amin with Cooper Interventional Radiology to talk about radioembilization of the liver (Y90). She suggested Robb have Y90 of the left lobe of his liver which is where "the cancer seems to have made itself quite comfortable – we need to give it an eviction notice." One week after his appointment, he was being mapped for the procedure (not the most pleasant way to spend the day). And the allergic reaction to the contrast dye was just joyous. Nothing like a dose pack and Benadryl to make a diabetic unhappy. At least it handled the hives and itching. Poor guy. He would forever need a steroid prep before any procedure with contrast dye. Well isn't that exciting? NOT! Poor guy couldn't catch a break. And neither could I. We were in this together.

One week later, on May 6, 2018, he was having Y90 to his left lobe. No big deal right? Shouldn't be any big reactions. WRONG! They said the first ten days were the worst – the most crucial – after that it would be smooth sailing. They put him on antibiotics and oral steroids. Well how exciting for a diabetic! Nothing like a steroid to drive blood sugar levels through the roof! Once again it was Judith Singley to the rescue. She helped us with pump settings and ways to try to keep Robb's sugars under control (which was no small task).

The first couple days weren't the most fun but the fatigue was the worst of it. That and having to stay away from each other. He wasn't supposed to touch any of us and I was supposed to sleep in a different room. 'Bout that. Instead, I made a blanket wall so he wouldn't roll on my side. There was no way I was going to sleep in another room when he was feeling so yucky and his blood sugar levels were all over the board and he was dying – like we were at the last ditch efforts to keep him alive. I had to be there to hear if the alarm sounded so I could get him to treat or run and get him juice if he was crashing. Just don't tell the doctor, okay. And I prayed over him. Over and over and over him. I just wanted God to heal my husband. Why wasn't he healing my husband?!

By day three the searing pain set in. Like Robb was being burned from the inside – which he was. Pain medicine took the edge off but the pain didn't go away. He was doubled over on the floor. The fatigue got worse. His blood sugars were crazy from the steroids he had to take. He was pretty miserable, but we had hope that this was burning the life out of the tumors in his liver. Thank God for good medications.

Two weeks to the day after the procedure he developed a fever. He refused to go to the ER (he was a stubborn Scot and a pig-headed German after all). I finally convinced him to at least see the doctor at MDA Camden. They examined him, did bloodwork, and asked a million questions. We were convinced he had an infection. Bloodwork showed no infection. The fever was from the radioembolization. They had assaulted his liver and his liver didn't like it very much. At least it wasn't an infection! Whew.

He finally was feeling better from it all and the oncologist decided to try oral chemo while we waiting for a clinical trial to take him. Robb's body didn't love the oral chemo. In fact, it caused some shortness of breath and lightheadedness. So they took him off for a week. Just to see if he resolved – which he did. Whew. He went back on. He had a pretty bad reaction (or so we thought). He almost passed out two days in a row. His blood pressure fell dramatically and he was so lightheaded that he thought he would fall. He was sweating and could hardly hold his own weight. I wanted to call 911. "NO!" Robb managed to growl at me. So I called the oncologist who agreed to see him in the office since they know what a stubborn Scot and pigheaded German he is.

The life of the caregiver often means being 'the bad guy' in order to get the person what they need to feel better.

The Fun Never Ends

Back to the doctor who promptly sent us to the ER "just to be sure it isn't cardiac". At the ER they ran tests and did a scan to rule out a pulmonary embolism. Not PE. Thank God. But they saw something they didn't like and wanted to do more testing. Something with his heart. And of course admitted him. He was thrilled. Do you believe me? No? Well, what would you believe?

When Robb goes inpatient, I go inpatient. We were in the ER, on a gurney in the hall, in plain sight of every fun thing that happens in the ER of the biggest hospital in the nation's most violent city. It was like our own private showing of 'Cops'. At least it was entertaining.

There we were. Pretty scared and very tired. They moved him out of the mayhem and into a different section. Less people and I had a chair to sit! It's the little things that mean so much. They were running tests until 1 AM. I was completely exhausted. Robb could lay and nap in the bed. I was sitting on a little plastic chair. I begged God to get us into a room. Finally they gave us a room. Thank you God! But when we arrived at the room, it had not been cleaned. So we waited in the hallway, in the middle of the night, completely exhausted, until the team came to clean. Finally – at 2 AM – he was in the room in bed. Of course there was nowhere for me to sleep. I asked for a recliner – I was told there wasn't any, so I sat in a plastic chair and tried to doze. At that point I was so tired, so hungry (I had not eaten at all since dinner two days before), so overwhelmed, so lonely, and felt so defeated. And I cried. Sitting in the dark, in a plastic chair, in a hospital room, in Cooper Hospital, looking at my husband who was sleeping - who was dying - and who seemed so far away, I cried. I poured out my heart to God. Out came all the fear and anger I had been pressing down for so long. It all boiled over. I told God how badly I wanted Him to heal Robb. I told him how scared I was and that I didn't want Robb to suffer. I told him how angry I was that He wasn't doing what I wanted – didn't He listen to our prayers? I begged God to heal Robb. I begged Him for some comfort and something that would give us – me – hope. I desperately needed some hope and it didn't help that I was so overwhelmingly exhausted. I sobbed. I felt completely alone. I don't ever remember feeling more alone than at that very moment in time.

You have kept count of my tossings; put my tears in your bottle. Are they not in your book?
Psalm 56:8

Surely the bottle of tears was quite large......

3 AM I started to feel like I just couldn't take another minute. My head throbbed, my throat was swollen and sore from crying, my body ached from that chair, I was exhausted but couldn't sleep

sitting up, I was at the very end of my rope. So God handed me more rope. Yep, apparently I hadn't learned my lesson. I had been telling God what I wanted but not what I needed. So I quickly tied a big knot in the end of that rope and told God I needed sleep and I needed it now. With that a nurse came in with a recliner! She had seen me crying and had gone to another floor to find me a recliner. I was so thankful. I wiped it down with sanitizing wipes and laid it back. And slept. For about 45 minutes before a nurse woke me to take Robb's vital signs. Then I slept again. For about 20 minutes before a nurse woke me to take Robb's blood. Ya, this is how it went. But it was much better than sitting in that terrible plastic chair. And the recliner was right next to Robb's bed so I could reach out and touch him. I could hear him breathing as he slept and I felt assured. God had given me what I needed. Not what I wanted. What I needed. I felt ashamed at how I had acted earlier.

I had another heart to heart with God.

Me: God, thank you so much for providing for me when I needed it most. I'm so sorry I acted like that earlier. I was so overwhelmed by the whole situation and everything we are going through. I'm so sorry. Please help me to be better at this. Help me to stay positive and just get through all of this. Please lead us to healing for Robb. If not in this life, then in the next. Take away his pain and suffering. Please God, please.

Then God put a song in my head, Overwhelmed, and it spoke to me. God spoke to me through this song. Robb's cancer was overwhelming. My life was overwhelming. What God was telling me was overwhelming. I felt God speaking directly to me as I listened to the song.

Big Daddy Weave. Lyrics to "Overwhelmed". *Love Come To Life: The Redeemed Edition,* 2014, https://genius.com/Big-daddy-weave-overwhelmed-lyrics.

[I encourage you to look up the lyrics and listen to the song. Apparently, it's not legal for me to quote the lyrics without permission from the owner of the song.]

Then He put another song in my head, "Trust In You" by Lauren Daigle. As God spoke to me through the words to the song, I was being told to let go of my dreams and lay everything at His feet. Let Him take control. His plan is better than my plan and I just needed to rest in Him. I had no idea what exactly was to come, but I had to completely trust in God.

Lauren Daigle. Lyrics to "Trust in You". *How Can It Be*, 2015, https://genius.com/Lauren-daigle-trust-in-you-lyrics.

And so the rest of the early hours passed with one praise and worship song after another popping into my head. God was giving me the comfort, the peace, and the support I needed through the songs that I loved with the words that I needed to hear. Then God put a thought in my head, *Write down all of your experiences, your thoughts, your fears, everything. Write it down in a book that will help comfort other caregivers and show them your faith journey.* As I sat sipping terrible hospital coffee from a styrofoam cup, thinking about all that had happened, hoping I had some concealer in my bag to help cover up the dark circles under my eyes, it came to me – Coffee, Concealer, and Conversations With God, A Faith Journey. Our faith journey. My faith journey. I was always a believer. I always had faith in the one true living God. I thought my faith was strong. When my faith was tested, I learned how weak I really was and the circumstances made my faith grow. God used these terrible trials to help me grow as a Christian, to be a better daughter of the King. He wasn't done with me yet. Little did I know just how much He would grow me.

Heartache (It's a play on words)

Mid-morning the doctors came in and told us the not-so-great news. Robb was not having a reaction to the oral chemo, he had a fairly serious cardiac condition and would need more testing. *Oh, great, one more thing.* They said he could be released *(praise God)* and do the testing outpatient. He had some things wrong and his heart was only working at about 35-40%. He had fluid buildup which meant he had symptoms of congestive heart failure and would require additional testing to know just how significant all of the issues were. He would need to follow up with the Cooper Cardiology Heart Failure Clinic. *WHAT? Was this really happening?* Don't press down the fear – pray through it. Rebuke that fear – but it kept popping up again. Pray. Pray some more. Lean on God. Lean harder.

Side Note:
Funny thing about pressing down the anger, the fear, the grief, when you hold it in too long, it ferments. Which is bad. Because eventually it explodes like a cork popping off of a champagne bottle and everything bubbles up and pours out – uncontrollably. I did a lot of that during Robb's battle. I pressed down the anger, pressed down the fear, pressed down the grief, and just kept going. That didn't go well for me. In fact, it caused a lot of really ugly physical issues for me. And, it all would come bursting out at very inappropriate times with a complete inability to reign it back in until it had all spilled out. Ugly….. I was starting learn to acknowledge my anger, fear, and grief, and would allow myself some time to be sad and cry. I wouldn't let myself get pulled into the pit for long though. When I 'wallowed' in it too long, it pulled me further in. I would set limits for myself to prevent the wallowing and sinking. I would purposely go to the store or make a call, anything to get my mind in a different place. I didn't dwell on my pain because the evil one used that as a snare for me. I had to decide to hold tightly to The One who indwells (The Holy Spirit). Some days are easier than others. Some days are a struggle.

Back to the story......
Well, okay, what does that all mean for his cancer treatments and overall health? Good question. We didn't like the answer. It meant he had to have more testing. Then a heart catheterization to determine if he needed a stent. The cardiologist said he would get the heart cath pre-authorized by the insurance and would do it as soon as the authorization came through. He suspected about a week. *Really God? Is this really the plan? What now?!* Don't be afraid – pray. But I was afraid! Ok, pray. Give it to God. Pray. Pray some more. Learn to lean harder.

This Train Is Out Of Control – Or Is It Just Out Of OUR Control?

The same day we met with the cardiologist and found all this out, we also had a follow-up appointment with Interventional Radiology. Dr. Amin said she wanted to do the right lobe of the liver. We discussed the new cardiac diagnosis and all that the cardiologist wanted to do. Having a stent placed would mean no other invasive treatments could be done for at least six months (because of the medications Robb would need to be on). Not knowing if he would have a stent or not, she wanted to do the Y90 before he had the heart cath. She picked up the phone and called Dr. Ginsberg (the cardiologist) on his cell. They decided she would do the Y90 asap and then he would do the heart cath as soon as the day after. She then called the lab that prepares the thingies they put in the liver and asked how she could get an expedited batch. Within minutes all was arranged and Robb was to report to Cooper Hospital at 6 AM two days later to have radioembolization of the right lobe. Wow, the train was moving faster...... God's hand was again evident in the timing of the diagnosis, the appointments, and the ability to coordinate the two procedures to maximize the possible outcomes. Only God could have so skillfully coordinated these things. God, the ultimate multitasker. Now, if He would just take away the cancer, the heart condition, the pain, the side effects, and the absolute terror that we lived with daily. That would be awesome. But it's not what I prayed for. Instead, I prayed for God's will, according to His plan, and in His perfect timing. Every time those fears would creep back in, I would take every thought captive to the obedience of Christ (*We destroy arguments and every lofty opinion raised against the knowledge of God, and take every thought captive to obey Christ. 2 Corinthians 10:5*)

The radioembolization of the right lobe was just as exciting as it had been of the left lobe. At least this time we knew what to expect. It didn't make it any easier for him. Or me.

Five days later we reported to Cooper Hospital for the cardiac catheterization. No big deal they said. It would only take about thirty minutes from the time they took him in until they would come tell me everything was fine. We waited his turn, I kissed him and told him I would be praying and everything would be fine. Off he went. Thirty minutes passed. Then forty, fitty, sixty, ... After an hour and a half I finally stopped someone in the hall and asked if Robb was okay. They went to check.

Finally, a doctor came in. He sat down and nonchalantly said, "Well, he needed a stent placed. It's a good thing we caught it in time. If he had a heart attack, and it was inevitable, it would have killed him." My world started to spin. *Was he serious?* The doctor went on to say that he had two tandem 90% blockages in "the widow-maker" – that they stented with one long stent. And he had a lesser blockage in another spot that they did angioplasty and were able to resolve. *Wow.* Robb would need to be on medications for six months to a year. He should be okay. Follow up with the cardiologist. *He should be okay? Should be? What is that supposed to mean? Did the doctor not read Robb's chart? He's dying – like we are just seeing how long we can keep him alive waiting for God to swoop in and do His healing thing.*

Robb was finally brought back to the room to recover. I told him what the doctor had said. He was visibly shaken by the news. Neither of us could believe he hadn't had symptoms prior to this. There really wasn't any warning. *Thank you God for saving my Robb. If it weren't for the 'chemo reaction' we never would have known and he would have died from a heart attack. Your plan God! Thank you for Your plan!*

(Part of) God's Plan Revealed

I had to contact the doctors at Columbia and let them know about the new diagnosis and recent events. The doctor said, "Well it's a good thing they found that. If he had been in the trial before it closed, he would have probably had a heart attack and he would not have survived it!" Wow. Those words hit hard. God's plan. Close the door to the trial, get other treatment that may help press the hold button on the liver tumors, try oral chemo that 'caused a reaction' that sent us to the ER that allowed the doctors to identify and treat the cardiac condition, keeping him from having a heart attack and dying. The IR doc contacting the cardiologist and working out the timing of the treatments and procedures. The lab being able to make a 'stat batch' of the thingies for the liver for the Y90 treatment. Catching the blockages before it was too late. Wow. It had to have been God. There are no other reasonable explanations for how this all fell into place. Hand of God. That's it. Trusting in His plan and praying through the fear.

Robb was admitted to the hospital overnight for observation. Of course I went with him. This time I insisted on finding a recliner. Although his diabetes caused a bit of a scare, with Judith Singley's help it was managed. We both slept, sort of, in between the nurses waking us every couple hours for vitals. The next day we were discharged.

To The Heart of the Matter

Follow up with the cardiologist – cleared for oral chemo. Back to the oncologist and June 2018 he started back on oral chemo. This latest adventure excluded him from more trials. Things were beginning to feel a little crazier. The side effects from this chemo wasn't as bad as the infused chemo, but they did last the entire time. Every day and night, 24/7. Not the best when you are already feeling weak and a little defeated. So we prayed. *Your will God, according to Your plan, and in Your perfect timing.*

New Vows

Our oldest son RJ got married on September 1, 2018. July and August were spent preparing for the wedding (a wonderful, joyful distraction). By the wedding week (he married a woman whose family is from India so it's not a wedding day – it's a wedding week), Robb was really not doing well and we had to decide which of the events he could attend. He was able to go to the Sangeet (just google it – it's like a big talent show with food and dancing – totally amazing and I've decided everyone should have one lol), the rehearsal dinner, and the wedding. Thank God he made it to the important parts! Things were looking 'iffy' the night before the wedding. He was really bad and we were awake most of the night. I wasn't sure I could get us both dressed for the wedding in time and pack all the right stuff to help him hold up for the very long day. God is good and provided Robb with the strength and stamina (and medications) he needed to get through the day and enjoy himself.

God also provided some amazing family members who took over 'watching' him and making sure he was okay, had what he needed, drank water, ate when his sugar was falling, etc. so I could also enjoy the day. Of course, I kept a watchful eye and covered for him when he wasn't looking so great. Thank God for the mini pharmacy I carried in my purse. Without the good medications he never would have lasted the whole day.

As I watched our son and new daughter-in-law exchange vows, I couldn't help but wonder if they really fully understood the promises they were making. Was Calla willing to change RJ's diapers? Was RJ willing to hand feed Calla and stay up all night for days on end tending to her if she was seriously ill? I pray they will never find out.

When Does It End?

When does this all end?! That was a question always in my head, but I was afraid to let out. His belly pain was getting worse with each round of chemo. By early November 2018 it was constant. He was feeling so DONE with it all. So was I. The CT scan showed more growth – lots more. The CEA (the cancer marker in his blood) had jumped to over 700. The oral chemo wasn't working so he had to come off of it.

I read hundreds of trials and investigated every one that might possibly accept him. I contacted all the major cancer centers in the United States asking if they had anything for which he might qualify. The answers were all the same. No. Or, yes, but the trial is full and they already have a long waiting list. Sigh......

In and out of the hospital. Always ICU. Weeks at a time. We had dubbed him 'Felix the cat' – but he had way more than nine lives.

I tried to talk about hospice care with him, but he would not admit he was dying. He insisted there must be a treatment out there that would save him. I knew there wasn't, and I knew that he was only putting himself through more pain and more side effects. My heart was breaking. I knew......but I didn't want to say the words out loud.

Open A Door That Cannot Be Shut!

No chemo had worked so far (26 months of various treatments). He'd been in and out of the hospital, had so many physical issues that they couldn't do more systemic treatments because it would put too much stress on his already stressed kidneys. Then the doctor told us that there wasn't anything more they could really do and that they were going "to focus on comfort care". Those words kicked me in the stomach. So we cried. And we prayed. We told God we were still looking for a healing in this life. We texted all the pastors. One of them came right over. He talked, read The Word, and prayed.

We prayed that God would open a door to healing that could not be closed. We had already experienced so many open doors that quickly closed in our face. We needed healing and we needed it quickly! Little did we know how that would all play out.

Three days later, I was calling 911 because Robb was bleeding - everywhere. If I wasn't paying attention, I might have missed God's hand that was evident in the whole scene and all the days that followed in the ED, ICU, and the oncology floor. But I was looking. I was always looking for God's hand.

The squad that responded wasn't our neighbor. That's actually a blessing. It would have been horribly embarrassing for a friend to arrive and have to help Robb half naked and bleeding everywhere onto a gurney and to the hospital. It was a squad from another town - filling in because our local rig was busy on a call. God's merciful hand.

Not long after the trauma team in the ED had done their cursory assessment and got Robb situated and covered (with lots of highly absorbent pads) a friend arrived - our son had let him know what was going on. He put on a jacket and drove to Cooper University Medical Center in Camden. After midnight. When he had patients to see in the morning. He didn't want me to be there alone if Robb died. I was convinced he was not going to make it. My brother and son who both saw the amount of blood (and humbly cleaned it all up) admitted later that they also thought the same thing. I would have needed that support if Robb hadn't made it. God's hand.

Once he was transferred to ICU the nurse let me stay in the room even though she was supposed to have sent me to the waiting area. I would have been sitting alone. In the dark. Crying. Instead, I was able to sit next to Robb's bed. In the dark. Praising God and asking Him for healing. God's hand.

That night, when I was finally leaving to go home (because they wouldn't let me stay the night), I couldn't find my parking garage ticket. I searched my handbag, my pockets, Robb's bag, everywhere. I was exhausted. It was Christmas Eve. My husband was not in great shape and in ICU. My life wasn't what I had expected. I said, "God, please show me where the ticket is!" I felt my pockets again and it was there. It had not been there minutes before. God's hand.

Leaving late that night, in the dark, I got on an elevator for the parking garage, a very creepy guy got on with me. As the doors were closing, I was just about to hit the door open button and get off when an arm appeared in the door - keeping the doors open. On walked a female nurse who looked more than capable of protecting both of us. She chatted with me. Got off on the same floor. Walked with me to my car and then to her car - right next to mine. She pulled out behind me and followed me all the way out. God's hand.

And so it continued. God was present every minute of every day. God was always with us. We just had to look for Him.

"Have I not commanded you? Be strong and courageous. Do not be frightened, and do not be dismayed, for the Lord your God is with you wherever you go."
Joshua 1:19

But he said to me, "My grace is sufficient for you, for my power is made perfect in weakness." Therefore I will boast all the more gladly of my weaknesses, so that the power of Christ may rest upon me

2 Corinthians 12:9

Not only that, but we rejoice in our sufferings, knowing that suffering produces endurance, and endurance produces character, and character produces hope, and hope does not put us to shame, because God's love has been poured into our hearts through the Holy Spirit wo has been given to us
Romans 5:3-5

Robb was finally released from the hospital, and we praised God for letting him come home. It wasn't the Christmas we hoped for. But it wasn't the Christmas I feared. We weren't done praying yet. We were praying for miraculous healing. If it was God's will, then it would be done. That was the change. The change that happened to my heart. God's will, not my own. I was resigned to the fact that Robb was not going to receive healing in this life. I was leaning harder on God than I had ever done. I had completely submitted to His will and handed over my husband to His Creator. *Your will Lord.* And I continued to ask for His will and praise Him for His hand that was and continued to be evident in our lives.

A week later, back to the hospital again. That time for over two weeks! Like I said before, it was not the Christmas we hoped for, but it wasn't the Christmas I feared. Yes, feared. I still had so much fear. I was learning to trust but still had 'those thoughts' jump up and grab me by the throat. Trust and fear cannot coexist. I knew that. Now I had to figure out exactly how to permanently evict the fear and sign a lifetime contract with trust. God was working on me. Hard.

Even though there were some really crazy scary things happening, God was with us, providing for us, showing himself present in every minute.

We had a wonderful nurse in the ED, Ashley. She tried to make Robb as comfortable as was possible. He was there for hours and hours and his back pain was almost unbearable. Even the pain meds weren't working. The ED gurneys are the worst - especially for someone with cancer in their bones and herniated discs! Ashley ordered a regular hospital bed for him. Once he was in that bed he was so much happier. It was a small thing, but evidence that God was guiding the medical team to do what Robb needed.

The hospital was full. Robb was supposed to go to the oncology floor so I could stay. No such luck. He was placed on a med/surg floor. I wasn't permitted to stay.

I drove home in tears. Sobbing to God to please keep him safe. The next morning I texted him. No answer. I called. No answer. I called the nurses station. No answer. I continued trying to reach him the whole time I was getting dressed and ready. I raced back to the hospital.

Although visiting hours hadn't started yet they did let me in. I arrived at his room as the tech was taking his blood pressure. Yikes! Way too low! She wrote it down and walked out. Really? She was unconcerned. I tried asking him why he hadn't answered but he seemed really out of it. He hadn't eaten - no way to order breakfast without a menu and phone number. And the phone was far from his reach. No one had offered to help him either. He admitted having "staggered to the chair but fell back into the bed". What? He had been up unassisted? And he fell?!

Suddenly he was very dizzy, almost out of breath, thought he was going to vomit, said he couldn't hear me and could hardly see, and couldn't seem to stay upright. I rang for the nurse. The minutes ticked by but no one came and he was getting worse. I ran into the hallway and called for help. "Is he ok?" a tech asked casually. "NO!"

I screamed. "Which is why I rang the bell that no one has answered! He is dizzy, can't hear and can't see! Can you please get help?!!!!"

Everyone started running. Blood pressure and oxygen were way too low. Nurse arrived and immediately got him on oxygen, called the doctor, and did a full assessment. I started telling her the whole situation. She had not been told most of his issues during report at shift change. Perfect. Too many patients per nurse, I know, but this was not just any patient – this was my husband and he was dying. Get it together and treat him!

We prayed for a compassionate nurse and He sent us Victoria. She was immediately on top of the situation providing calm yet swift care, and always going above and beyond to get Robb what he needed. She pressed for a critical care evaluation. It was God's leading that directed her actions. She was an obedient servant.

I prayed God would protect him. Off to ICU where he spent seven days.

Acute renal failure. Very low blood pressure. He was swollen with fluid and was HUGE all the way up to his chest! Tests. Scans. More tests. The first set of labs came back as possible infection. I felt like my heart shattered right there. I was sure this meant the end. They said things like, "this is very serious", "likely an infection", "looks like septic shock". That would have been catastrophic. They started him on heavy doses of IV antibiotics.

Our oldest son RJ, remember he's a physician, talked to the doctors in their doctor-speak. He maintained a calm demeanor and I assumed everything would be okay. As we were walking out to the parking garage together that evening (they booted me out at 9 PM every night) he asked me about my finances. He wanted to know about things which he had never asked before. Is there a mortgage on the house? How much is the payment each month? How much life insurance is there? Do I have any savings? How much is the pension, and will I continue to receive it even when Robb was gone? *HOLY COW! HE THINKS ROBB IS GOING TO DIE! SOON!* I answered what I could, but my mind was swimming. *Is this really the end? After all the times God allowed Robb to live through things that surely should have taken him?*

I almost panicked. Almost. I had my moment, and then leaned harder on God. I got into my car and started to drive. I was sobbing. I called my sister Karen (on speaker phone) and I was crying so hard that she couldn't understand what I was saying. I had to explain that Robb was dying of sepsis and his organs were shutting down. I told her he needs prayer – now. I reached out to everyone and asked for prayer. I begged God to heal Robb – in this life as well as the next. I put out a prayer request - well, more like a plea. I said we would beg God that the test was wrong and there was no infection. God can.

I arrived home and dragged myself inside. God kept giving me support through hymns and praise and worship music. He told me to trust, so I did.

Alexa, play praise and worship music. Alexa responded, "Ok, here's a station for you, praise and worship, on Amazon Music." The first two songs that played were exactly what I needed to hear. Again. The two songs I needed most.

"Overwhelmed" by Big Daddy Weave.

Big Daddy Weave. Lyrics to "Overwhelmed". *Love Come To Life: The Redeemed Edition,* 2014, https://genius.com/Big-daddy-weave-overwhelmed-lyrics.

"Trust In You" by Lauren Daigle.

Lauren Daigle. Lyrics to "Trust in You". *How Can It Be*, 2015, https://genius.com/Lauren-daigle-trust-in-you-lyrics.

There they were again. The words I needed when I most needed them.

I didn't sleep much that night, but I prayed. I prayed harder than I think I had ever prayed before. Funny how each time there was something seemingly catastrophic, I drew closer, nearer to God, and I found that my prayers were deeper, more spirit-led than ever before. There is no limit to the depth of God's Word, no limit to the strength of His power, and no limit to the amazingness of His love.

Yes, amazingness is a real word. It's in the 'Conni Says' dictionary in my head.
Amazingness
uh-**mey**-zing-ness
noun
The quality or state of being amazing
See also *God*

I asked everyone to pray that the doctors were wrong and that Robb didn't have an infection and that his kidneys would start to work again. Hundreds of us prayed.

The next morning I was at the hospital bright and early. I always participated in 'rounds' when the team discussed Robb. I'm not sure the team liked it, but I wanted to know what they had to say and I wanted to offer input. I can be the doctor's best friend and worst nightmare – depending on the situation.

I had all of Robb records loaded onto my own private website. All of them. Every lab result. Every office note. Every test report. Medication lists, allergies, surgeries, procedures, everything. So, when I was there for rounds and the doctors suggested something

I knew to be incorrect, I brought up the results on my phone and 'shared it' with the team. When they suggested that the endocrinology team 'take control of his insulin' (ie take him off of his very snazzy state of the art pump and sensor that runs in auto mode and is the closest thing to an artificial pancreas as you can get on the FDA approved market), I explained how the pump and sensor worked and assured them that he would not agree to come off of it. Once endocrine knew what system he had, they agreed that his was far more effective than their method of finger stick hourly and treat accordingly. God's hand.

It was during rounds that I would be able to ask questions and get the information I needed to better direct my prayers. It was also during rounds that I would have an opportunity to share God with the team. I would tell them that we have masses of folks praying for Robb and for them – his treatment team. Our God is greater.

Two days later, the team confirmed they were wrong – there was no infection. Praise God! His blood pressure had been terribly low (likely caused by the diuretics and the cardiac drugs) which shut down his kidneys which caused more swelling. Once they could rehydrate his cells and increase his blood pressure (with medications), his kidneys began to make urine again. Yay! God's hand.

I was there every day helping with things that I never thought I would ever have to do. I washed him, changed him, helped him potty, changed his ostomy pouch, brought him food, filled his water, called for his meds, everything he could possibly need I took care of. It was my privilege because I love him. It was a gift I could give him – one that I continue to cherish to this day. I would want the same thing if the positions were reversed.

They couldn't figure out exactly why his body was in shock. He still had trouble maintaining a good blood pressure. He was retaining so much fluid but they couldn't give him diuretics with low blood pressure. More tests. More 'ologists' weighing in. He had started to improve. He was finally able to be on oral instead of IV meds. He was transferred to the oncology floor for another five days. I moved in with him of course.

There was one test that would tell us if he required some very long term IV medication and would cause a long hospital stay. He just wanted to go home. He wasn't permitted to leave the hospital until the test came back negative - it was far too high a risk that he could have a catastrophic event. Thursday morning the preliminary result was 'weak positive' and they had to send the sample to an outside lab for the next part of the test. The test results would take 3-5 days. And we would have to stay in the hospital until they came back. Then we would have to stay another couple weeks (if it was positive). I almost panicked. Almost.

I put out another prayer plea - ask God for the final result of negative be done today. God can. I didn't care that the results were supposed to take 3-5 days. I knew that God could. That's what we needed at that moment. We needed to get Robb home.

That afternoon at 5:30 the doctor came in to tell us they just got the results back and it was negative! He said the results are never done that quickly. I told him God can. By 6:30 we were leaving the hospital! Our God is awesome!!! Yes God can!

Buy Nothing

When the doctors started talking about being able to go home. They told us the things we would need to have at home. Robb's condition had worsened, and we needed a walker, commode, hospital bed with the better mattress for back pain, 2XL clothing (he was retaining a

TON of fluid from poor liver and kidney function), depends, chucks pads, rinse-free wash and disposable washcloths, and lots of lotions for his extremely dry skin. How was I supposed to get all that in a day or two so he could come home? And how was I supposed to be at the hospital taking care of him and also out shopping for all that stuff? And how was I going to pay for it all? Sigh.......

Then God reminded me of the free-cycle Facebook group called Buy Nothing. I was a member of our local one so I posted an 'ask' on the page and listed everything we needed. Within a few hours we had EVERYTHING we needed and more! Usually we have to go pick up the items from people's houses, but this time they all delivered to our house. I was so touched by the outpouring of love!

So, when we arrived home, we had everything we needed and more!

Home Sweet Home

Finally, we were discharged, and we could go home. Aaahhhhhh... Home. Exactly where we wanted to be. Where we needed to be. Robb wanted to be in his own recliner, watching his own big screen TV, with his favorite oversized heating pad on his back, with his dogs Sparkie and Isabelle on his lap (they are only 10 pounds each so they both fit nicely on his lap – and help keep him warm), with his favorite blanket (really soft and snuggly), sipping on his 'blue water' (sugar free powerade), having me bring him his meds (and food if he got hungry), and napping when he wanted. Home. No better place in the world. I agree.

The bliss of home was short-lived. The onslaught of visiting nurses, home PT, and home OT began. Every day there was at least one of them coming to the house and making Robb get up and do things that exhausted him. The slightest thing exhausted him. His condition was quickly declining.

Bad to Worse

The doctors had told us that there was nothing more they could do except keep him comfortable. The only way to keep him comfortable was to give him lots of painkillers and let him rest. But he wanted to keep trying to find a way get well. It was heartbreaking to watch him struggle with the pain and try to push through his exhaustion in order to prove he wasn't dying. I knew better. Caring for him alone became impossible for me. He had swollen so large he could hardly walk, couldn't bend his legs, and couldn't toilet himself. His mental state had deteriorated. He was hallucinating and often couldn't form a clear thought. Things were really bad.

When the visiting nurse came in, I told her I just couldn't do it alone anymore (meaning I wanted to get the visiting nurse to arrange for an aide to help bathe and dress him). I also told her about his mental state and that I had contacted hospice to inquire about their services. She didn't think he needed hospice yet and insisted something more could be done. She took it upon herself to call the oncologist and told him Robb needed to go to the hospital to be checked for an infection. She convinced Robb he should go.

I was furious! Why would she put him through this again? It was clear he didn't have long. Couldn't she just leave it alone and let the poor man live his final days in peace?

Back to the hospital we went. A long wait in the ED before getting a wildly uncomfortable gurney in the hallway. My nerves were shot. I was doing everything I could to keep him comfortable all the while I was dreading the inevitable long day and night ahead of us. Labs were drawn. CT was done. X-rays taken. Hours later we were moved to a room in the ED. They did a rectal exam – he was bleeding again. He was so swollen and hadn't urinated in since the morning (over twelve hours). They wanted a urine sample. Not sure how that was supposed to happen. It took me and a very patient nurse who was willing to take direction (I had done this a couple times before), working together to try to get a Texas catheter on him. Let's not go into details, but understand that when someone swells like that, to that extent, *everything* swells, and I do mean everything. Making it impossible to find the parts necessary to properly affix said catheter. Soooooo..........

All the test results were finally back, and the very young resident came in to talk to us. They wanted to keep him. They wouldn't be able to give him his dilauded (the only pain medication that worked) because it affected his liver and they didn't want to further damage his liver. *Seriously? His liver is riddled with cancer and he's dying! Why won't you just give him the pain medication he needs to be comfortable? What is wrong with you?!* They thought it might take a couple days to determine whether or not they could help reduce the swelling and correct the renal failure. *What? Are you kidding me?! In a couple days he may be dead!* I asked the doctor about going home. He said it is certainly our choice but that he didn't know how long ..... if he went home. I asked for a few minutes to discuss with Robb. I prayed for the Holy Spirit to guide my words.

The doctor left the room. I turned to my very sick husband who couldn't formulate a clear thought and could not focus on the reality I was about to tell him. "Robb, we have two choices. We can stay here and they can try to figure out how to help you. It will involve more tests, more labs, and they will not give you your pain medications because it will affect your liver. They will give you tramadol. Or, we can go home and they will make you as comfortable as possible and you will have your own chair and your own TV and I'll take care of you. Robb kept saying, "I don't know what you're saying." And "what does that mean?" I finally had to say, "You can stay here and they can try to make you live a little longer but with tests and labs and without pain meds, or we can go home with your medications and you can be comfortable in your own home for whatever time you have left." He kept saying he didn't understand and that he couldn't focus on what I was saying. When I said, "Two options – stay here with no meds or go home with meds." His response completely floored me. "I want the option where I live!" I burst into tears. "I do too, sweetie, but I don't think that's in the cards."

He was crying. I was crying. I tried to calm him by assuring him that he would be with Jesus in Heaven. Again, another response that completely floored me. "Do I? How do I know that?" I cited scripture. I asked if he believed in God. Yes. Does he believe God sent his only son Jesus to die on the cross for his sins? "Well, yes, but how do I know it was for my sins? I don't think my faith is strong enough." I fell apart. Completely fell apart.

There I sat in the ED, holding my husband in my arms, not knowing why I hadn't known before that he was questioning his faith. I called Pastor Chuck Mitchell. No answer. Followed by a text that he was out to dinner for his son's birthday. I called Pastor Jeff Kliewer. He answered. I'm not sure exactly what I said, but I know I explained the situation through tears and asked if he would talk to Robb. I handed the phone to Robb. I only heard Robb's half of the conversation. Jeff was clearly telling him about what the Bible says about being saved. Then Robb was saying, "Jesus I believe in you, help my unbelief." He was repeating it over and over. As he did, he went from sobbing to calm. He finally was listening intently and then handed me the phone. He asked me, "So what's it like on the other side?" Again, I fumbled for some scripture but my brain was almost as unfocused as his.

The doctor came in. What had we decided? I looked at Robb clearly expecting him to say he would go home. Instead, he said he would stay. Wow.

Wait for hours before we were off to the floor. 1 AM. This time it was a private room (so I could stay) but not on the oncology floor. It took forever for a bed to arrive (there was literally no bed in the room). I had to go hunt for sheets and a blanket. I got him settled but he was clearly in pain. I did everything I could to get the meds he needed and kept asking for anything else they would give him. Poor guy! Then I put on my sweatpants and looked for a recliner to sleep in. Nope. There was a broken chair for me to sleep in. How lovely.

They woke him (consequently me) every 2 hours for labs. He was able to go right back to sleep. Me, not so much. As I laid there feeling annoyed by the whole thing and praying that God would make this better, the thought occurred to me – this was to assure Robb of his salvation. This was all orchestrated by God. God is the ultimate multitasker and had arranged everything so that Robb would talk to Pastor Jeff, and Jeff would rely on the Holy Spirit for the right words. Nothing would be okay – my husband was going to die and probably not long from now. But everything would be okay – my husband was assured his place in Heaven and he knew it. God's hand. God's will, according to His perfect plan, and in His perfect timing.

The morning came. Robb's pain was worse. The teams of doctors came in and out, each with a different plan and different tests to be done. His pain got worse. Now he was literally writhing in pain. I told the nurse I needed pain management here now. She left the room. In walked another intern from the medicine team. I tried to explain the situation and told him we needed pain medication. He told me no. They could not do that because it processes through the liver. I lost it. In my very calm (sounding) adult 'business' voice, I explained that Robb's liver was full of cancer as was the rest of his body. That I wanted the pain management team here now. He left the room.

I turned to Robb and explained that if I tell them he wants to go home on hospice they will give him pain meds. He said, "Then I want to go home." I was relieved and horrified all in the same millisecond. This was really it.

In walked the pain management doctor. It was Robb's pain management doctor! He was the one on call that day! I explained the situation and within minutes he had administered liquid dilauded and Robb was out of pain. He fell asleep. I told him that Robb wanted to go home on hospice. Today. He tried to tell me it would take time to get everything arranged. I told him I already have everything I need at home and told him whole long tale (well, I did give him the abridged version). He left, made a couple calls, returned and said it was all arranged.

Robb was asleep. After we discussed the home medications I asked, "How long?" Another response for which I was not prepared. "Days." He said he was sorry and asked if I would be ok. Although I shook my head yes, what I really meant was, "NO I WON'T BE OKAY! YOU JUST TOLD ME MY HUSBAND WOULD BE DEAD IN DAYS!" He gave me a hug and told me he would check in later when we got home.

The social worker asked if I could get him into the car and then into the house myself. Well, um, no. He can hardly walk five feet let alone go up steps! I made a few calls and sent a few texts. Within minutes LeeAnn Parry and Kim Parry Jones had arranged for help. If we could get him into my car, there would be people waiting at my house with a transport chair and they would carry him into the house. What a blessing! God's hand.

Home Again

We were off. Driving home it started to snow. It was like a blizzard. The snow was blowing so much that I could hardly see. It suddenly occurred to me that there had been significant precipitation on every major event in my life. Every one. The day I was born there was a snowstorm. The first day of school it poured rain. My confirmation it poured rain. My graduation from HS it poured rain. The first day of college it poured rain. My wedding it poured rain. The birth of each son it either poured rain or snowed like the dickens. Here I was bringing my husband home to die and the snow was so bad that I couldn't see the road.

By the time we arrived home it had slowed. The guys were so sweet and so kind to Robb. They helped get him out of the car (not an easy task) and then carried him in the chair up the steps and into the house. They helped him into his recliner and chatted a few minutes with him. How wonderful they were!

Then they left and it was just us. He slept. The hospice nurse arrived to do the intake. I was so confused why she was asking about services that wouldn't start for about a week. I told her the doctor had said he has only days to live. I assured her all we needed was the pain management kit with all the liquid medicines so I was sure I could keep him comfortable.

The Parade

The next day was full of visits from social worker, the chaplain, the pastor, family members, and on and on. It was a never-ending revolving door. Everyone suddenly wanted to be here now that they were sure he was dying soon. I was a little bitter that people weren't seriously interested in coming when he was sick and needed company (and when I needed company). Now suddenly everyone had to come all at once.

So I went about cooking, putting out snacks and food, getting out drinks, and entertaining. All I wanted to do was sit and hold my husband's hand and talk with him. I knew we didn't have much longer together. Instead, I had to entertain so that everyone else could have their last words with him. It was wonderful that so many wanted to be there to visit with him, but I wanted every minute to myself and our kids. I know that sounds selfish. I suppose it is.

Anthony was able to get leave, and they drove up from Virginia with our two week old granddaughter Aubrey. When Robb found out they were coming, he rallied. It was as though he was holding on until he could see them. It was amazing!

Anthony ran in the door holding the car seat, scooped out Aubrey, and laid her in Robb's arms. He melted. And so did I. Robb was instantly in love. We had the weekend with them and the other kids. It really was perfect.

Until Saturday night when Robb's rectal bleed started again. I had to have the boys help me get him into bed. His oxygen level fell drastically, and he needed to be on oxygen. He needed the head of the bed raised or he couldn't breathe. He was bleeding quite a bit and I thought this was going to be the end. I tried to stay calm and assured the boys it would be fine.

He asked me to clean him up because he was soaked with blood, and the diaper, and the chucks pads, and sheets - all soaked. His ostomy pouch was full of blood. I waited until the boys went to bed. It was late Saturday night. I called hospice and explained the issue and said there was no way I could do this myself. He was just too big (swollen with fluid) and there was way too much blood. The nurse told me they don't come out to help change patients. I was crying and told her the severity of the situation. She said she was sorry, but she couldn't send anyone.

Now What Do I Do

I was so frustrated by the situation, but I put on my big girl panties and started gathering supplies and assessing the best way to tackle this problem. Water basin with warm water. Gloves. Lots of new chucks. Clean sheets. Clean shirt. New diaper. Disposable washcloths. Rinse free cleanser. Ointment for his bottom. Snack tray to put the supplies on. I couldn't roll him, hold him, AND clean and change him myself. I had to wake Matthew. Poor guy. Between us we got him all cleaned and changed with fresh clothes and sheets, and lots of heavy-duty chucks pads covering every inch of the bed and doubled up where it counts. I gave him his pain meds, tucked in his blanket, and kissed him goodnight. I laid down on the sofa hoping for a couple hours sleep before he would need more meds. Sleep didn't come. I was up with Robb. He was needing medicine.

Then needed the bed lowered. Then raised. Then wanted water. Then...... and so it went all night.

Sunday was a little bit better day until Anthony and Andrea left with Aubrey. Through tears they waved goodbye knowing that would be the last time they saw Robb this side of Heaven. Although we didn't give birth to Anthony, and he doesn't have our last name, he belongs to us as much as our other three boys RJ, Andrew, and Matthew. Aubrey is the only grandchild Robb will have ever held. We all knew it. And we are so grateful they were able to come up before he died.

It was Sunday night, February 3rd. Robb was having a terrible day. He was agitated, having pain that required more frequent doses of heavy-duty pain killers, and had started hallucinating. The liquid dilauded had never arrived. Apparently, there was a shortage and nowhere in the tristate area had any. I called the doctor and asked what I was supposed to do. Crush the tablets, add a tiny bit of fluid, use a medicine syringe (no needle) to administer between cheek and gums if necessary. He had gotten to the point that he couldn't swallow a tablet, so I was giving him the meds every hour or two this way just in the back of his mouth. He seemed stable. I knew things were getting bad.

Matthew and Andrew were there. RJ and Calla arrived after RJ got off work. I was completely spent. I hadn't slept more than an hour or two in days. I hadn't eaten. I couldn't even concentrate. I had to keep a list of medications with the times I gave them and when they were due again. I couldn't keep track any more. My brain just wouldn't work.

I had a small meltdown and RJ told me to go lay down and get a couple hours sleep. I argued but he assured me he would take care of Robb. I showed him all the meds and the tracking list. I kissed Robb and went to bed.

I woke up about 4 hours later. The house was quiet. I got up to check on things. Robb was asleep in the hospital bed in our living room. RJ was dozing in the rocker next to him and Calla was dozing in the recliner. Matthew was asleep in his room down the hall and Andrew was asleep in the recliner in the back room. I told RJ and Calla to go home and get some sleep. I would be okay. After they left, I kissed his cheek and sat in the rocker holding his hand. I dozed on and off.

When the labored breathing started I crushed the pills and put them between his lip and gum. That seemed to help. I kissed his cheek and sat down in the rocker again. I realized I was shaking. I knew what was happening and I couldn't stop it. I had begged God to heal my husband, but here he was in a hospital bed in a coma getting ready to leave this life.

I had told Robb many times that whenever he felt done fighting, if things were just too much, he should go home to Jesus. We talked about how I would manage and what we had (financially). He had asked the boys to take care of me and they all said they would. I finally said, "God, he's yours. I give Robb to you. If you're not going to heal him in this life, please heal him in the next. Please take away his suffering." I kissed his cheek and closed my eyes. I listened as his breathing slowed.

I couldn't seem to focus on one thought. My mind had so many thoughts all at once. Every one of them made me feel like I was being ripped into pieces. I was 55. He was 57 – one month shy of his 58th birthday. We were supposed to be traveling, going out with friends, going to small groups at church, and having the time of our lives! Instead, Robb was dying in a hospital bed in our living room, I was sitting next to him completely helpless and eternally heartbroken.

I realized I was timing his breaths. Waiting. At 5:24 AM, February 4, 2019, Robert James Murray, Jr. breathed his last breath on this earth. I kissed his cheek and said, "I love you," one last time. I waited. I couldn't seem to move. I sat. Holding his hand. It seemed like an eternity. I was memorizing every detail of his face. I didn't want to believe it was real.

Then I got up. Folded the blanket I had around me. Woke the boys. I felt the tear all the way to my soul. And burst into tears.

And the two shall become one flesh. So they are no longer two but one flesh.
Mark 10:8

Then the man said, "This at last is bone of my bones and flesh of my flesh; she shall be called woman"
Genesis 2:23

The whole "two become one" and "flesh of my flesh, bone of my bone" thing is real. I didn't realize just how real until I felt the tear. It was as real a pain as if someone had ripped a bone from my body with their bare hands.

The boys went about the business of calling people. I sat. In the rocker. Holding his hand. My brain wouldn't fully accept what had happened. I cried. I was both relieved that his suffering was over and devastated that he wouldn't be here with me ever again. I didn't want this to end.

At first, I had been so sure God would heal him. I know God can. I didn't understand why He wouldn't. Why He didn't. *Why? WHY?* That's what was swimming in my brain.

"It's like having a personectomy." That's what my cousin Pam said when I told her how badly my heart hurt. She understands what I was (and am) going through. She lost her husband to heart disease at a young age. A personectomy. An involuntary personectomy I might add. That pretty much describes it.

I know that Robb is in a far better place, that he's no longer suffering, he's completely healed and living in the presence of Jesus! Praise God for that! I also know that one day I will join him there. Praise God for that! It's the "left behind" that is the harder part. Thankfully God is with me here too.

Robert James Murray, Jr.
3/18/61 - 2/4/2019

On February 4, 2019, after a 28 month battle with stage 4 colorectal cancer, Robert J. Murray, Jr. "Robb" received perfect healing when he went home to his Savior.

Survived by his loving wife of 33 years Constance S. Murray (née Hare), his sons and daughters-in-law: Dr. Robert J. Murray, III & Dr. Calla Vodoor Murray of Philadelphia PA, Andrew D. Murray of Moorestown, Matthew D. Murray of Moorestown & Katherine Lodato of Cinnaminson, Anthony L. Phelps, IV & Andrea Mott Phelps of Dahlgren VA, and granddaughter Aubrey Lynn Phelps. Also survived by sister Deborah Bell (Tom) of Middletown NJ and brother Scott Murray (Nancy) of Howell NJ, brother-in-law William D.Hare

(Stephanie) of Moorestown, sister-in-law Karen Hare Eder (Keith) of Riverside, father-in-law William H. Hare, Jr. of Moorestown, as well as many nieces and nephews, cousins, and close friends.

Robb was the middle child of Robert J. Murray, Sr. & Barbara L. Murray (née Dawkins). He was raised in Wall, NJ where he was a cub scout, played little league, ran track, and played HS soccer. He played the trumpet in the Wall HS band and was the chief crew member of Tice Racing at the Wall Speedway. He attended Brookdale Community College, transferred to Trenton State College and in 1985 graduated with a degree in Technology Education.

In 1986 he married his college sweetheart Conni Hare. Together they raised three boys, adding an adult child to their family after their boys had all graduated high school. A handy guy, with the help of family and friends, they completely renovated two houses - first in Maple Shade and then in Moorestown.

He worked at two schools before landing at Lenape Regional High School where he taught for 30 years. He brought the video media program to Lenape High School and it quickly grew into the studio broadcast run by students. He taught video media technology, photography, digital photography, woodworking, electronics, technology today, and CAD. He treated his students with kindness and respect. He believed every student had value and that there were no bad kids, just good kids who sometimes made bad choices.

Robb loved to hunt and target practice, but his favorite thing was spending time with his family. He coached his son's sports teams all through school spending every spare minute with them on the soccer field, baseball field, lacrosse field, and on the side of the pool cheering them on when they swam for Sunnybrook Club as little guys. He was so proud of each and every accomplishment. He was a youth leader at church and an active teacher participant of the

Fellowship of Christian Athletes at school. He was a great man who considered everyone extended family.

He enjoyed woodworking and was always working on a project making furniture and home decor. In July 2015 he and Conni opened Barrel of Murray's, LLC, an online store selling home decor made from reclaimed wine and whiskey barrels and shipping pallets. As things were just starting to really take off for them, he was diagnosed with stage IV rectal cancer already metastatic to liver and lungs. The chemo caused so many side effects that his woodworking was sporadic and the business slowed. He was hoping his sons and others would help to keep his dream alive after his passing into glory.

Although Robb had always been a believer, it wasn't until faced with death that he truly understood the promise of eternity through Christ Jesus. He and his wife Conni started writing a book about the faith journey they were on. Know that the final chapter is not a sad one. Although Robb's earthly body lost the battle with cancer, he ultimately won the fight. The final chapter is a joyous one where Robb found perfect healing and ran into his Savior's arms.

Viewing Friday Eve 6 - 8 pm at the Cornerstone Church, 515 Mt. Laurel Rd., Mt. Laurel, NJ 08054. Funeral service Sat. 10 am at the church. Interment will be private.

Robb specifically asked that people do not send flowers to his viewing or service. He said flowers are pretty for a time but they do no good in the world. He wanted people to donate to the Moorestown and Lenola EMS squads or the American Cancer Society for colorectal cancer research.

Please be sure to designate your donation as a memorial contribution in his name so the family will be notified of your contribution.

Lenola EMS Squad
229 N. Lenola Rd., Moorestown, NJ 08057

Moorestown EMS Squad
261 W. Main St., Moorestown, NJ 08057

American Cancer Society

Three of the boys spoke at the funeral. I was impressed by what they said. I'm so proud of all of our boys.

RJ Murray

On behalf of the entire family I would like to thank you all for coming out and supporting our family and celebrating the life of my father.

To be honest, my dad and I were never that close throughout my life. We didn't hug or say I love you. We would just give each other a strong handshake. Luckily, that changed in the past few years and we did become very close. He did teach me many lessons throughout my life. He taught me how to shoot and hunt. He was there when I shot my first deer. He taught me how to throw a ball and play sports and was there coaching us through all of them. He taught me how to give a proper handshake and look the person in the eyes. He taught me how to do yard work and how to perfectly mow the grass so that the lines were perfect by lining up the wheels on the previous track mark. He taught me how to get up and rub some dirt on my cuts and bruises and to just "walk it off". But the biggest lesson that he taught me is how to be strong in the face of adversity.

I still remember that day sitting in the King of Prussia Shake Shack and I got a call from my mom who was very concerned because my dad had not gone to the bathroom in a few days despite a literal ton of laxatives. I know that is probably more information than any of you would like but it's my speech so deal with it. My first question to her was "when was his last colonoscopy"? She said that he had never had one. At that moment, deep down, I knew. From there she took him to the emergency room and "dad's wild ride" took off.

The amazing thing was that he remained so positive throughout the entire experience. Every time that I saw him, he had a huge smile on his face. Mom would always text me and update me and tell me how much pain he was in that day. But when I got there none of the pain seemed to matter. He asked Calla and I about our day and our lives and how the wedding planning was going. He didn't let the cancer dictate his life. He got to go to Gettysburg and Boston. He got to see my engagement and wedding. He got to see his first grandchild thanks to Anthony and Andrea. And the first time that I can remember hugging my dad in quite some years was at my engagement party and last week for the first time in decades, my dad and I said that we loved each other. I am forever grateful that that was able to occur.

Stuart Scott once said that "When you die, that does not mean that you lose to cancer. You beat cancer by how you live, why you live and the manner in which you live". And I think that the way my dad lived and how he lived these last few years, he didn't lose. He did not let cancer dictate his life. So, I toast to you dad, the man who beat cancer. Slainte.

Andrew Murray

You know how when you're little you argued with other kids about who's dad is stronger than everyone else's? Well, my dad actually WAS stronger than everyone else's. And I didn't really realize it until the very end.

Back on October 17, 2016, I came home from work and there mom and dad stood in the kitchen. They said they had to talk to me. I thought "oh great...what did I do now...". But then they started to tear up and I knew something was really wrong because dad NEVER cried, remember...because my dad was obviously stronger than everyone else's...I mean did ya see the calves on that guy?

Sorry, getting back to the story, so dad told me that they got his tests back and found out he had cancer. So many things started running in my head but then I thought, "who cares? Thousands of people have cancer and they all lived and beat it. Dad can too because he's so strong!"

Well as we went on living life and going to treatment after treatment after treatment I thought "see he's still got it and doesn't even seem to be affecting him". But as time went on and tests started coming back that it was getting worse, I started to see his health decline. He knew his time was coming to an end.

The last few weeks of his life it seemed like he was in the hospital almost every other day. We knew it was only going to be a few weeks. But even though he was in obvious pain, I'd come home from work and ask him if he was doing alright and his response was, "yea, why?".

Then the last time he was in the hospital and his tests came back, we realized that his cancer became way worse than it was just 2 weeks prior. Now instead of a few weeks, it's a couple days. You could see the fight in him just diminish. His health started to just go downhill much faster. He slept all day and was never really happy, but who can blame him?

I quickly called Anthony, who if you didn't know is dads adopted son. Anthony and his wife Andrea just had a beautiful little baby, Aubrey. Dad loved getting pictures of her and really wanted to see her but the doctors told Anthony and Andrea that the baby shouldn't travel until she had all of her shots. I begged them to see if there was any way that they could get here. Well, God pulled through and the doctors said they could come see him. When dad heard the news, his health somehow got a little better. He knew he had to see them so the fight was back on!

Friday night they arrived and the very first thing they did when they walked in the door was put Aubrey in dad's arms. He instantly fell in love. He lit up and had a big smile for the first time in a while. He got to see his son and his very first grandchild. Then once they left, his health went right back down. He gave all the fight he could just to see them. They were the last ones he had to see and say their goodbyes.

On the last day I sat with him almost the entire day even though he wasn't awake. He wasn't really responding to anything or opening his eyes. When he did it was because he wanted to just sit up and dangle his legs off the side of the bed. He was begging to do it but the nurse said he was on too many meds. He got real upset at that.

Later in the day I noticed him opening his eyes wide, looking off to his right (there was just a wall there) and he'd lift his hand like someone was standing right next to him holding his hand. After a couple times I realized it wasn't just because he's going crazy, but his angels were standing right there with him holding his hand.

RJ and Calla came over after work and the three boys watched him while mom finally got a little sleep. While she was sleeping, us three boys said "who cares what the nurse said...if he wants to sit up, let him sit up". So with all the strength we had, we sat him up and held him there. I was in the back holding him from falling back, RJ and Matthew were standing next to him holding him from falling forward. After 5-10 minutes of sitting there he lifted his head and said "ok, I'm ready". At the time I thought he meant he was ready to lay back down in bed, but now looking back, he really meant he was ready to go home. He saw that he could count on us to be there for mom so that nothing would happen to her.

A few hours later, mom got up and now it was her turn to watch him while we got a little rest. He waited until it was just him and her to go home. He fought to stay here while his boys were around him. Even in his last minutes, he was still fighting to protect us.

And THAT is why my dad is obviously the strongest.

Anthony Phelps

I'm Anthony – the adopted son.

Words will never have enough meaning to describe Robb. He opened up his house to me when I had nowhere else to go and reestablished what it was like to have a home. To always show support and love when life just wasn't working in my favor. To tell me how proud he was of the man I've become knowing the crazy kid he saw growing up.

But for me, the greatest gift was seeing Dad hold Aubrey, a memory she'll be too young to remember but one I will never forget. I only wish he could have watched her grow and to tell her all about her amazing Mommom and crazy uncles. To smoke cigars on the back porch and laugh about whatever was on our minds after a few beers. But that's just my worldly selfishness, because Heaven is far greater than all of that and I know he's still with us in our hearts.

A memory that stands out the most for one crazy reason was the summer before I shipped out. Matt, Andrew, and I were cutting the grass and for some reason we thought it would be funny to do donuts on the lawn tractor. Well Dad wasn't too keen on us doing that and gave us a stern talking to about being responsible. But we couldn't help but laugh at our immature boy tendencies. Don't worry Dad, we won't do it anymore, we promise to cut straight lines from here on out. But if anything breaks just know it was Matt because he's the youngest.

Put in a good word for all of us Dad. God knows we need it.

Pastor Chuck Mitchell

Robb was the favorite teacher, filled with grace and loyalty to his students; Mr. Murray quickly became an institution at Lenape High School, where anyone and everyone, those who were quiet and those who appeared to be difficult, were all drawn to him; because he was humble enough to know that all had worth and value. He, of course, went above and beyond with teaching mass media, where he initiated the morning show, establishing other classes around the art of media, and taught life lessons, believing that his students could and would accomplish anything. He had a profound impact on students and teachers because he believed every student had value and worth, that all children were created in the image of God, who sometimes made bad choices.

He was a woodworker. There is a cross that hangs on my front door, from a whiskey barrel. He was real about his faith, utilizing normal items to speak about a deeper message. Robb was a coach. He was an initiator. He was a leader. His legacy will continue live and breathe life into others. He is adored by his wife; celebrated by his boys. He was real, raw, and with that smirk, laugh and smile.

For Robb, appreciating the Jewish High Holy Days, would easily look forward to Rosh Hashanah, "Rush Me Homie," so he could return home sooner to be with his family. Family was more than important and significant to Robb; family was vital, whether through blood or simply strangers becoming quickly friends, who remain for a life time. A life time. A life time is not measured in years; a life time is measured by an impact. Not just you, all of you, seriously look around, how wide and deep his impact has been: teachers, students, friends, church families, extended family, adopted sons and daughters, brothers, sisters, Conni, RJ, Matthew, Andrew.

Robb is my friend, will always be my friend. When Robb was squeezed by his circumstances, who Robb was, and who God created him to be, became evident in his life. In Proverbs 18:24 *(The Message)*, "Friends come, and friends go, but a true friend sticks by you like family." In Proverbs 17:17, "A friend loves at all times, and a brother is born for a time of adversity."

Robb was "always" **accepting**, no matter where you were in relationship with God in Jesus, no matter where you were in relationship with him. Robb always **loved** you right where you are; knowing that the love had its source in Jesus. He always **understood** that everyone had a story that influenced how they reacted to life. Robb was always quiet, introspective, and always said what needed to be said only when necessary. Even with questions about faith, Robb knew that he could ask those questions and remain faithful to God. Robb remained a steady, influential support and influence in many of the lives that are here.

He has had an impact; had an impact on me. Robb is my friend. I love Robb Murray, and everything that he is and always will be. I will miss my friend, his strength, his courage, and his willingness to remain until he knew that his boys would care for their mother, his wife, and where he and his wife of 33 years, his partner that he met in college and knew that she would be the one, could have their final moments together. I will miss my friend, my kilt wearing, smirking little Scotsman. I will miss Robb.

Hymn – Amazing Grace

Psalm 23 was read by Katie Lodato (now Katie Murray)
The Lord *is* my shepherd; I shall not want.
[2] He makes me to lie down in green pastures;
He leads me beside the still waters. [3] He restores my soul;
He leads me in the paths of righteousness for His name's sake.
[4] Yea, though I walk through the valley of the shadow of death,
I will fear no evil; for You *are* with me;
Your rod and Your staff, they comfort me.
[5] You prepare a table before me in the presence of my enemies;
You anoint my head with oil; my cup runs over.
[6] Surely goodness and mercy shall follow me
All the days of my life; and I will dwell in the house of the Lord forever.

Revelation 21, 22 read by Calla Vodoor Murray
[3] And I heard a loud voice from the throne saying, "Look! God's dwelling place is now among the people, and he will dwell with them. They will be his people, and God himself will be with them and be their God. [4] 'He will wipe every tear from their eyes. There

will be no more death' or mourning or crying or pain, for the old order of things has passed away."
[5] He who was seated on the throne said, "I am making everything new!" Then he said, "Write this down, for these words are trustworthy and true."

[6] He said to me: "It is done. I am the Alpha and the Omega, the Beginning and the End. To the thirsty I will give water without cost from the spring of the water of life.[7] Those who are victorious will inherit all this, and I will be their God and they will be my children.

Then the angel showed me the river of the water of life, as clear as crystal, flowing from the throne of God and of the Lamb [2] down the middle of the great street of the city. On each side of the river stood the tree of life, bearing twelve crops of fruit, yielding its fruit every month. And the leaves of the tree are for the healing of the nations. [3] No longer will there be any curse. The throne of God and of the Lamb will be in the city, and his servants will serve him. [4] They will see his face, and his name will be on their foreheads. [5] There will be no more night. They will not need the light of a lamp or the light of the sun, for the Lord God will give them light. And they will reign for ever and ever.

Message – Pastor Jeff Kliewer

NOTE: Robb and I talked about the service before he passed. He wanted Jeff to give a salvation message at his funeral. He didn't want anyone else having to go through a traumatic illness not knowing for sure where they were going when their life on earth ended.

Robb Murray Funeral
"Jesus I believe; Help my unbelief"
Mark 9:24
Preaching Notes

Bartimaeus had never seen a miracle. He was blind. He used to beg by the roadside near Jericho. He couldn't see but he could hear and he could cry out. People tried to silence him. But he cried out all the more, "Son of David, have mercy on me!".

Have you ever thought that if God showed you a miracle in Jesus' name, you'd believe? Would you believe if God had healed Robb in the here and now?

Faith came by hearing. Bartimaeus never saw a miracle before He cried out for one.

Blind Bartimaeus did two things well: listen and cry. Imagine the desperation.

Christian funerals have two purposes. One is to mourn the loss of a loved one. We remember his life. The other is to proclaim the hope we have.

Christian witness is nothing more than one beggar telling another beggar where to find bread.

Main Idea: This morning, because this is a funeral (God did not choose to heal Robb in the here and now, even though we asked a lot), I take as my task to answer two questions. Why listen to Jesus? Why cry to Jesus? I'm going to tell two short stories.

1. Why listen?

   1. Mark 9:7 **Listen to Jesus** because the Father says to listen. "This is my beloved son. Listen to him." Why do you have this incessant need to talk? Why do you think your ideas about how to approach God need to be heard?

2. Mark 9:1-13 **Listen to Jesus** because Jesus makes Himself the issue. The glory of Him. "looking around they no longer saw anyone with them but JESUS ONLY". Don't tell until I rise from the dead. They ask about ELIJAH. He answers with a question, "And how is it written **of the Son of Man** that **he** should suffer many things and be treated with contempt?"... "The Son of Man is going to be delivered into the hands of men, and they will kill him, And when he is killed, after three days he will rise." (9:31)... ""For even the Son of Man came not to be served but to serve, and to give His life as a ransom for many" (Mark 10:45).

3. **Listen to Jesus** because He is either Lord or some kind of Liar or Lunatic and he's not the latter. Die and rise language PLUS the I Am's.

4. **Listen to Jesus** because He alone has the backing of the Law and prophets. Mark 9:8, the issue is JESUS ONLY Mark 9:12 They are preoccupied with Elijah, but Elijah is not the issue. Yes, that was really cool, but he was only there to show that all the prophets testify of JESUS.

2. Why cry?

1. **Cry to Jesus** because He can sympathize with even the worst pain. Mark 9:17 "I brought my son". He can sympathize because He suffered too. The Father turned His face away from His own Son, to save us. But LISTEN. The love of the Father was such that He gave His beloved Son. He restrained His emotional desire to rescue from pain. It was for this purpose: to atone for sin. While we were yet sinners, Christ died for us. Consider the raw emotion of this father.

2. **Cry to Jesus** because He makes life meaningful. Marx said "religion is the opiate of the masses". It is more than an opiate. Faith in Jesus makes this world the opposite of what it is without him—meaningful instead of meaningless.

3. **Cry to Jesus** because fragility and weakness do not repulse Him, but attract Him. The fact that he heard the disciples is all the more reason to listen to Jesus. Arguing about who is the greatest (still happens on the basketball court and many areas), failing to cast it out, Churchill said history is written by the winners. But the disciples always present themselves with reality. The women were the first to find the empty tomb. On the road to Emmaus, they were not believing the women, "some women amazed us"

4. **Cry to Jesus** like Robb did because ASSURANCE comes from raw honesty. The fact that you are crying to Him is indicative of mustard seed faith. And he will not despise it! And a wounded reed he will not break off. And a smoldering wick he will not snuff out. Are you concerned about your faith in Jesus, whether or not it is strong enough? That concern is a good sign. Robb Murray, when he came to die, listened to Jesus and cried to Jesus. He gained assurance by praying over and over "Jesus I believe, help my unbelief"

So, I say, listen to Jesus and cry to Jesus. Believe what? What did He say? No, exactly what? 1. The Person of Christ 2. The work of Christ (He told them in Mark 9, "The Son of Man is going to be delivered into the hands of men, and they will kill him. And when he is killed, after three days he will rise." Mark 9:31) 3. According to the Scriptures (There is no basis for anything Christian without God speaking and preserving) 4. Forgiveness of sins and eternal life 5. repentance and faith (I am happy to be honest with you and tell you that you must take up your cross to follow Jesus. There is an entire road to life that will be revealed to you once you have the LORD. Walk with Him)

Closing Bible story: Two men went to the synagogue. One was there to listen and cry. The other heard without ears to truly listen. Which one will you be today? Pray out loud with me with the desperation of the helpless father, the desperation of the blind beggar, the desperation of the sinner beating his chest, the desperation of Robb Murray, "JESUS I BELIEVE, HELP MY UNBELIEF". We'll repeat it several times.

Hymn – Victory in Jesus

Eulogy by former student and good friend Scott Juffe

Today we gather to pay tribute to Robb Murray. I prefer not to mourn the life lost, but to celebrate the life he had.

Back in 1993 I was sitting in Middle School English and given a list of elective courses to pick for the following year, my freshman year at Lenape. There was woodshop, and auto body, and all the typical stuff. Somewhere along the list I found this one class, TV/Media Production. That sounded so cool to me, I immediately picked it without question. Little did I know I wasn't just picking a class....I was picking something that would have a profound impact on my life.

Webster's Dictionary defines teacher, as one who instructs. Robb didn't just instruct. He supported, guided, encouraged, and enabled his students. This isn't called teaching, it is called mentoring. Robb loved what he did and never hesitated to encourage or foster a student who showed interest.

There were plenty of memories about that class. I remember having to make a music video...mine was set to the Flintstones movie. Each student operated a different piece of studio equipment for another student's video. If you ever watched The Goldberg's, picture 20 Adam Goldberg's all making their own videos. Poor Robb, he had to endure watching these videos being made, then again to grade them. Tylenol and a bottle of Jack....I mean passion and dedication to your students had to be what got him through that.

I remember the formation of "The Morning Show" to kick off the 1995 school year. Robb would come in early so that we could get everything ready to be on the air by 8 and stay late so that we could produce segments. He let the students run everything once we showed we could do it. I remember when he came to me and asked me to produce a weekly segment from the show. He wanted something spotlighting the different kids around the school. The rest was up to me. I took it and ran with it, made it my own work which is what Robb wanted every student to do.

Peeling back the layers, there was more to Robb than what he did at Lenape. There are a lot of people who thought highly of Robb. I'm not talking about those who thought he looked good in a kilt either. Although if I must say he did wear it well and wear it proud! Robb was the proudest Scotsman I know.

Robb also had a profound appreciation of the Jewish High Holidays. You might be scratching your head, wondering "Jewish High Holidays"? He's not Jewish? To Robb Rosh Hashanah was Rush Me Homie which meant he could get home sooner to his family. Family was very important to Robb. Robb was an active part of his family's life, from coaching his kids in various sports, to actively supporting them in their activities.

They say if you want respect and kindness you have to earn it by showing it to others. Robb did this as respecting people was part of his core. It was evident at the fundraiser with the sheer amount of people who came out to support Robb. It is evident again today by the amount of people who have shown up to give their final respect.

The values that Robb held as a person made him a truly wonderful person. While we might be burying Robb today, we aren't saying goodbye. We are simply letting him into another part of our lives. It's the part we where we remember and embrace a truly great man. Everyone here is here because Robb made an impact in part of your life. If we take that part and reuse it; the world will be a better place. Robb will always be with us in our hearts and memories.

A letter from a former student the day after Robb died:

I hope this helps you! I do hope this helps you memorialize your husband even better. He was a wonderful man and we're so grateful for the time we had with him.

My freshman year of high school, I was placed in Mr. Murray's homeroom as well as his photography class. We connected so quickly, and I was introduced to the morning show, broadcasting, and the film/tech arts. I went from being gung-ho for criminal justice to mass media and I really owe that to my favorite teacher. Every year of high school after that was spent in his homeroom as I joined the morning show program and headed it up with Mr. Murray. We had so much fun, I learned SO much, and I went to him with just about everything.

My junior year is when my little brother entered high school with all of his own issues to be dealt with. He was running with all the wrong crowd, skipping classes, doing drugs, and getting into fights and it was extremely frustrating for everyone. We were afraid he'd end up in jail, be expelled, or maybe even die from drugs young if he didn't get help but he listened to nobody and ran away every time we tried to force him to help himself. His second semester, he joined Mr. Murray's drafting class. Mr. Murray immediately identified him as my brother and as a result, always gave him the benefit of the doubt. One day my brother got into a big fight and Mr. Murray finally sat him down for a man-to-man talk. It would be an understatement to say that that talk was a turning point for my brother. He really took what Mr. Murray said to heart, which was confusing, but exciting to my parents. The fights stopped, he cut out some of the bad kids, he quit the harder drugs, and over the next semester we really saw massive, positive changes in him. We give pretty much all the credit to Mr. Murray for getting through to that kid when no one else could.

For the rest of both our high school careers, we looked upon Mr. Murray as a second father, going to him with any problems just for advice, or seeking him out to say hi at any given time of day. And when my sister entered high school two years later and immediately joined the morning show crew, it all came full circle as she saw him every single day too and kept the connection alive even after my brother and I had graduated high school AND college.

Mr. Murray was an institution in and of himself, an amazing man whose presence changed every single one our lives for the better and you should know that even years later, we appreciated him and recalled the things he taught us. No visit back to Lenape was ever complete without going to his classrooms and saying hi to our favorite teacher. We're so grateful for the time we spent with him.

Photo boards displayed at viewing and funeral

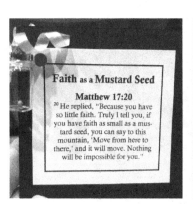
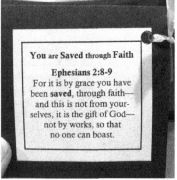

Distributed at the funeral to all attendees.

LESSONS LEARNED

Tomorrow Isn't Promised

Don't put off until tomorrow what you can say and do today. Tell people you love them and how much they matter to you. Be there for them. Show them how much you care. No matter how awkward or uncomfortable you feel doing it – just do it! You will quickly get used to saying the words and you will never regret it.

Share the gospel of Jesus Christ. Tell everyone. EVERYONE you meet. Tomorrow isn't promised for any of us. What if the person you tell is led to faith and repentance today and then passes tomorrow? They are saved because you shared God's truth before it was too late!

Anxious for Nothing is Harder Than You Think

It's completely human to have anxious thoughts and feelings of fearfulness. It's what we do with them that matters. I had a hard lesson to learn when my life was consumed with those thoughts and feelings. My circumstances justified them (in an earthly sense). It wasn't until I learned to surrender them to God – fully surrender them – that I could find peace. God's peace. I would give them to God, and then I would sneak over and take them back to hold them for a bit. Then I would realize what I was doing and give them back to God. Then…you guessed it – repeat. I had to learn full surrender – fully trust in God's plan – in order to find peace. Once I learned to release the anger, release the fear, release the worry, release the anxiety, and relinquish the control, I could find peace.

Do not be anxious about anything, but in everything by prayer and supplication with thanksgiving let your requests be made known to God
Philippians 4:6

Peace I leave with you; my peace I give to you. Not as the world gives do I give to you. Let not your hearts be troubled, neither let them be afraid.
John 14:27

And the peace of God, which surpasses all understanding, will guard your hearts and your minds in Christ Jesus
Philippians 4:7

I have said these things to you that in me you may have peace. In the world you will have tribulation. But take heart; I have overcome the world
John 16:33

Casting all your anxieties on him, because he cares for you
1 Peter 5:7

When you give your life to God, He takes you into His family and you become a cherished child of the Most High King! He has purpose for your days, and He invites each of us to join in accomplishing His will here on earth. He uses our storms, if we agree to step out of the boat, to grow our trust in Him, to grow our faith in Him, and to grow our relationship with Him. When you seek Him, you will find Him. He is nearer than your next breath.

You will certainly face storms in this world, but take heart, God has overcome the world!

Don't Sweat The Small Stuff

My mother's lengthy battle with multiple illnesses taught me to be a better daughter to my parents. My husband's battle with cancer, diabetes, and heart disease has taught me to be a better daughter of The Father. Someone recently told me that her chemo healed her cancer, but that her cancer healed her. I understand exactly what she means. I don't know that I would have understood prior to my own lesson.

When faced with serious illness, I suddenly became focused less on the little stuff like what's for dinner, what to wear, cleaning the house, buying groceries, etc. I used to be fanatical about the house if someone was coming over. Heaven forbid I didn't clean the bathroom at least twice a week. And groceries - well, my pantry and freezer were always full and I was always ready to host a group no matter the size at a moment's notice. Today, my freezer is rarely full and the pantry is often sparse (I know all the delivery places and who makes the best food for guests - just say'n). The things I focused on were doctor's appointments, treatments, medications and refills, organizing medical information, and trying to do everything in my power to make my husband's battle easier for him. More importantly, I focused my attention on the Great Physician and His will for our lives. The lesson - don't sweat the small stuff! Ya, I know, cliché. But true! The house will eventually get cleaned. If there's not enough to feed a crowd, ask the crowd to bring food or order out. If the laundry isn't done, wear something else - there's always something in the back of the closet I forgot I had (so what if I really don't like it and it looks icky on me - if it's clean, wear it). **Lesson – stop stressing about things that don't matter to eternity.**

I used to be focused on always having the perfect gift for every occasion and making sure it was wrapped to impress. When things got difficult, gifts became a dollar store card with a gift card or cash. Easy peasy! And no one complained or said how much they missed my artistic wrappings. **Lesson - people like cash and don't really care about the card anyway.** Eventually I was able to do my fancy wrappings again. But it's not what mattered. Sharing God's love is what matters.

Patience Is a Virtue (whether you like it or not)

Another much needed, but not necessarily wanted, lesson was patience. I used to say, "Patience is a virtue, just not one of mine." God grabbed me by the ears and taught me patience. NOTHING goes smoothly. Ever. I really was not prepared for the reality of navigating the cancer care network. Insurance companies with erroneous denials, health care providers billing incorrectly and then billing us instead of correcting the problem, providers insisting we pay our copay even though we met our out of pocket, trying to get provider's billing companies to refund the overpayments, people who were either incapable of actually doing their job or unwilling to try, phone call after phone call, email after email, typed letters, and it would take weeks or even months to resolve something that seemed to be an easy fix if people would JUST DO THEIR JOBS! I learned in a hurry that I had to simply stay calm, be patient, and continue to wade through the muddy swamps of the cancer care system. Every day brought more challenges, and more opportunities for me to learn patience. This is a lesson I'm still learning. Some days I'm better than others. The more incompetence with which I have to deal, the worse I get, the more likely I am to need a refresher on patience. God is always happy to provide said refresher. **Lesson – patience is a virtue** and if I don't learn quickly to be a virtuous woman, God will be happy to help me learn.

The Easiest Lesson - Love is a Verb

What do you think of when someone says they love you? What does it mean when you say you love someone? For most people it conjures up thoughts of romance, two lovers gazing into each other's eyes, Valentine's Day, and all the flowers and diamonds you can imagine. For others it means how you feel when you hold your newborn baby, the way your heart swells when you see your child's smile, or how elated you feel when your son or daughter comes home from college on break. All feelings.

I contend that love is a verb. It is the act of showing your love. It is the things you do that matter. Sometimes it's showing love even when (especially when) you don't feel it. When someone seems to be unlovable, love them harder. Show God's love. DO something to prove that all are worthy of God's love.

Selected Facebook posts from my personal timeline and my blog on this very subject:

<u>December 14, 2016</u>
You say "I love you" - prove it. Love isn't simply a feeling. It's a verb - an action. It's how we behave toward one another. "For God so loved the world that He gave His only son..." (John 3:16) God _ gave_ ... He did something to prove His love. "Greater love has no man than to lay down his life for another" (John 15:13). To _do_ something, to sacrifice, is to show love. It's not buying gifts. It's not diamonds or vacations. It's not toys. How do you SHOW your love? How do you prove it?

Conversations With God - A Faith Journey blog post
August 10, 2018
Love is a verb

How do you handle disappointment? What is your first thought or first reaction when someone hurts you (intentionally or unintentionally)? Do you go straight to anger? Do you yell? Do you say or do something to hurt back?

Too many people go straight to anger - they try to hurt back. If that's you - STOP! Take a deep breath and decide the best way to act upon your situation rather than react to it. Adults should not behave like four-year-olds. Adults are supposed to be rational and think things through. Adults are reasonable and kind. Stop acting like a child.

If you know someone who is having trouble adulting, love them through it. Help them to know how much better life can be if they can just stop acting like a child. Old habits are hard to break. Situations sometimes put us at risk for falling back into our old ways. Love one another. Love is a verb.

This became clearer to me over the years. I did so much for everyone. Sometimes I would get so upset that I was doing for everyone, and no one was doing for me! I have to admit, I did get really hurt. I got angry with God. I was only in my early 50's! We were *supposed to be* going out to dinner with friends, vacationing, having fun, enjoying each other! What *were* we doing? He would veg on the sofa while I took care of him, the dogs, the children's needs, friend's needs, and of everything. Cooking, cleaning, laundry, shopping, medications, appointments, treatments, managing his side effects, making him comfortable (as possible), making sure he had whatever he needed, helping the kids, helping friends and neighbors, always doing for everyone else. Even when I was sick, had a broken foot, or felt like taking a mental health day. Who was taking care of me? No one.

I shouldn't get upset. I know I shouldn't. But once in a while I would throw myself a pity party – party favors and all. Too bad no one showed up except me. That's when God gave me a boot in the tush, reminded me to look to Him for support, and to reach out to people who would help pull me back out of the pit into which I had willingly thrown myself. They showed me God's love and their love for me. I am thankful for that.

Just Do It!

When confronted with news that a family member or friend has a serious illness or is going through something difficult, our first instinct is to offer help. "Let me know what you need," "what can I do for you," "anything you need just call me." Well, I have to say, that when people say these things to me I would say "thank you so much, we will be fine". *You want to know what I really need? A cure for my husband. Sleep. My old life back. That would be a good start. Thanks for offering.* But my snarky answers were not from God, they were my frustration. Honestly, I often didn't know what we needed.

At first, I had no idea what I needed. I honestly could not think past the next few hours let alone think about what we might need in the next few days. I would take care of everything as it came along. I was running on autopilot.

As the weeks and months went by, I became acutely aware of what we did need. There is no way I would ASK for the things we really needed. And there's no way I would let anyone do the things we really needed. I couldn't say, "what we really need is someone to clean the house," or "maybe you could get a meal train going for two or three times a week", or "someone to mow the lawn or weed the garden would be awesome."

Don't say it - just do it! Meals are a blessing but not usually on the list of things to do until suddenly it's dinnertime and the care giver has to throw something together for the family. I was always so appreciative of people who cooked for us. Tell the person what day you will be delivering a meal. Don't have time to do it yourself? Order them take out.

Arrange with friends to be sure their lawn is mowed. Pay a service to mow their lawn. Weed their garden or pay someone to do it for them.

Anyone who has dealt with a cancer patient knows you have to keep the house more clean than usual because the patient is often neutropenic and far more susceptible to catching something. But there is usually little time to clean with everything else they have to take care of. I would have LOVED to have someone clean my house. I hate cleaning and I hated having to clean so often. I had so much on my plate already. And I had to find several hours each week to clean. With all the expenses, there is no way we could afford to pay someone to clean for us. But there was no way I was going to ask anyone to help me clean.

And the list goes on. It's exhausting just getting through each day. And being up much of the night with the patient makes it even harder to function as an intelligent human being during the day.

Don't ask – just do it!

Hide & Seek

Hey – where did everyone go? In the very beginning, many people came to visit, brought meals, called, texted, wanted to know everything that was going on. But as the weeks dragged on, most people went back to their lives and they stopped being involved in our lives. We had very little real meaningful support. Out of sight, out of mind. We often felt like we were playing hide and seek with many of our family and friends.

If you know someone going through something serious, please make it a point to stay in touch with them. Even a text message or a call every few days means so much.

People Like A List

So many people asked how they could help. People really do WANT to help, they just don't know how. So we published something on our private website and shared it on Robb Murray's Wild Ride FB page. **Use this as a guide for how you can help someone going through something life-altering as cancer.**

Ways To Help Robb Murray

On October 17, 2016, our father Robb Murray was told he had a large mass in his colon. This was the beginning of a wild ride....not one he would have chosen, but one that he will nevertheless take.

Robb Murray (aka Lord Murray the Kilted Celt) grew up in Wall, NJ, the middle child of Bob & Bobbi Murray. He graduated from Wall High School then attended Trenton State College (now TCNJ) where he studied Technology Education. There he met our mother Conni Hare. He graduated college and starting his teaching career. One year later he and Conni married. Since then they raised three wonderful, amazing, brilliant, handsome sons (yes, we are – oh, and humble, very humble), added a fourth equally wonderful amazing brilliant handsome son, and two adorable fur-babies.

In October 2016, at age 55, he had a routine colonoscopy (regrettably his first). The doctor found a large mass. Further testing was done and it was determined that he has stage 4 rectal cancer – metastatic to the liver. There are also affected lymph nodes in the abdomen and suspicious nodules in the lungs.

November 3, 2016 was the last day he worked, and he began chemotherapy November 9 at the MD Anderson Cancer Center in Camden, NJ. Two months later, in mid-January 2017, after scans showed the tumors were shrinking, he was scheduled to begin radiation/chemotherapy to target the rectal tumor in hopes of shrinking it so it could be more easily removed surgically.

February 2, 2017, just 3 days before he was to begin radiation, he experienced a complete bowel obstruction and was rushed into surgery to perform a colostomy. Three weeks later he began the radiation/chemotherapy which lasted for 6 weeks. In mid-April, 2017, new scans showed that his cancer had "gone crazy". There was regrowth of previously shrunk tumors as well as radical new growth of the liver tumors. The rectal tumor appeared to be unaffected by the radiation. Sigh. He announced his need to retire effective July 1, 2017 (although he had not actually worked since early November 2016). After 32 years of teaching. He was devastated, but he is in a fight for his life – literally.

The doctors changed his chemotherapy protocol to something even more aggressive. The side effects are pretty brutal. His type 1 diabetes only served to complicate matters and has made his ride a little more wild. He continued on this protocol until late March 2018 when it was determined that the treatments were simply not working. His tumors has grown and his CEA was skyrocketing. His treatments were halted and he was told to pursue clinical trials.

After lengthy investigations, doctors visits, records gathering, phone calls, and emails to practically every major cancer center in the USA, Robb was finally told that he was eligible for a clinical trial at Columbia at NYU. It is a personalized vaccine trial and has had astounding results in lab trials. But the day prior to his visit to the clinic the trial was placed on voluntary hold. Since he cannot wait too long with no treatments, it was suggested her pursue radioembolization of the liver to help control the liver tumors.

On 5/4/2018 he had Y90 treatment to the right hepatic lobe. The side effects were horrible but the CEA dropped 200 points in just 30 days! The trial was still on hold so he began an oral chemo. On days 7 and 8 of the new oral chemo he had some serious side effects and ended up being admitted to Cooper hospital in Camden, NJ. After having many tests it was determined that he needed a heart catheterization to determine if there was a blockage. They quickly squeezed him in for a Y90 treatment to the left lobe before having the heart cath. On 6/6/18 he had Y90 to the left lobe. On 6/13/18 he had a stent placed for a tandem 90% blockage and they were able to angioplasty another blockage. Wow.

He is no longer eligible for most clinical trials. We now have to pursue whatever trials we can find for which he is eligible. He is back on oral chemo, hoping it helps hold the cancer back while we wait for a trial.

As you can well imagine, this is an expensive battle even for people with 'good' insurance. Doctor copays (often 3 per week since 2016), medication copays (he is on over two dozen drugs that need to fill monthly), over the counter meds and supplies, durable medical equipment coinsurances (diabetic supplies, ostomy supplies, etc.), ER copays (when side effects take a turn for the worse), gas to/from doctors and treatments, parking, items needed for at home comfort during this, and the list goes on and on. Then there's Mom's lost time from work to take him to all of his appointments and to care for him when he's feeling really poorly. Their expenses have gone up dramatically but their income was cut by more than 1/3.

Many have asked what they can do to help. Several suggested a GoFundMe page. Mom and Dad don't like to ask for help. Mom keeps saying "We will be fine – we will figure it out." Mom is really opposed to making a GoFundMe page right now, so we decided to do this page instead. Please help as you feel led.

Ways To Help Robb Murray
The Best Way To Help:
Pray

Pray for healing. Pray for relief from the side effects. Pray for comfort for him and our family as he goes through the treatments. And pray for God's Grace through it all.

Cash, checks, and cash cards are appreciated for the many expenses related to his illness.

Drop off cash, check, or gift cards to their home

To make a donation electronically, you can send funds via PayPal

(link removed)

Gift Cards Appreciated To:

(list removed – local shopping for food, household items, gas, etc)

Gift Cards For Meals:

Dad likes to get take out when he's having a good day. Or pick up something on the way to MD Anderson Cancer Center when they know it's going to be a very long day of treatment. They don't get take out unless someone has given them a gift card.

Some of his favorite places are:

(list removed – list all takeout places complete with address and phone number – note if they deliver or not)

Other ways to help

Feel free to message Conni or one of us and we can discuss it with you.

Thank you to everyone who has already helped our family. You are all such a blessing to us.

RJ, Andrew, & Matthew Murray, Anthony Phelps

The Hardest Lesson

God sustains us through it all. Even when the very worst we can imagine doesn't hold a candle to what we are handed, God is with us. *How will I ever live without him?* That's the question that would plague my mind. It became my reality. As friends were posting about their trips and cruises, I was looking through brochures trying to decide on an urn for Robb's cremated remains.

What now? *What am I supposed to do now God?* He answered *Show people Jesus.*

God doesn't waste a second and He is the ultimate multitasker. He took all the heartache and pain and told me to use it to show people Jesus. I saw Jesus in every step we took throughout this journey. I watched as God opened His mighty arms and held us through it all. Now God will hold me as He guides me on in my journey.

THE MESSAGE

Friend, if you got this far and haven't stopped reading, then you know about one of the most difficult times of my life. You know how God made Himself known over and over, every minute of every day. He orchestrated our entire wild ride. He sustained me. He strengthened me. He was and continues to be my rock, my fortress, my all in all. If you are going through something rough (let's face it everyone does at some point in their life), you know how hard it is. If it weren't for God, I would be face down in a bottle of bourbon or worse. You know how God held me together and helped me learn what I needed to learn in the waiting and the suffering.

You also know that my initial prayers were not answered the way I wanted. We all need to understand that God is not a pez dispenser for prayer requests, and He answers every prayer – EVERY prayer – just not always the way we want. Sometimes God says no, or not yet. That's often hard for people to understand. God's plan is greater than our plans. His will is higher than our will. His timing is far more perfect than our timing. I asked God (well, no, reality is I begged and pleaded with God) to heal Robb in this life. God did heal him, but not in this life. God said no. I believed. I prayed. I read scripture and claimed a healing. I was absolutely certain that God would heal Robb in this life. I know He COULD do it. But He didn't. God healed him in the next life. The life that really matters. The life that goes on for eternity. This life is only a blink compared to our eternal life. We might live IN this world, but we certainly are not OF this world. We are just passing through on our way home. We will all live forever. Our eternal destination depends on our choice of whom to serve.

I struggled whether to add this next part or not, but my good friend Melissa Kehm (and my proof editor) assured me I absolutely need to add it. She said she always believed in God but didn't have a true understanding of Him and what is expected of us as believers. She didn't always fully understand how to let God into her life, and how to open her heart to the Holy Spirit to be her guide.

My good friend Lynn (who asked me to remove her last name) was my sounding board for how to write the next part. See, I was always a believer, my whole life, I never had a time in my life that I didn't believe in God. I had varying levels of relationship with Him, but simply lack the perspective of what it feels like to not believe and be faced with the choice to believe or not believe. She had a time when she was not a believer and then came to know Christ as her personal Lord and Savior. When I asked for her input and perspective, she said this, "If I were faced with the notion of burning in hell and having to repent, and not knowing why I was doomed to hell (simply stated), or what repent means (beyond the fire and brimstone definition I have heard all my life), it would turn me off completely. I just know what it was like to live in oblivion and then be faced with what seemed like judgement of lifestyle and a sentence of eternal suffering without understanding what it all meant. The Gospel IS offensive [to those who don't yet believe and don't yet understand], but hard things don't need to be harshly delivered. There is an urgency in witnessing [telling people about God and the good news of Jesus Christ], as there should be, but there should be a balance of willing investment of a total stranger's eternal destination and the finesse of speaking to them as if you were Jesus Himself.

Robb was a great guy (just ask his former students). He was involved in youth activities and pointed herds of kids to the Cross. He went to church. He knew who God was, yet it wasn't until the gift of suffering entered his life that he finally came to KNOW God and understand that all along, salvation was for him as well. Robb's waning health and impending exit from this world stirred his spirit to accept the invitation he had ignored all of his life (and didn't even realize it). I praise God for the illness that ultimately drove Robb to seek God's will for his life ... an eternity with his Creator."

Basically it's Sin & Salvation for Dummies:

We will all live forever. Whether you believe it or not, you really will live forever. First, we live in this life here on earth, then, when this body dies, we move on to our eternal life. This life doesn't last very long, but it's during this life that we need to decide where we are going in the next life. Tomorrow isn't promised for any of us, so you need to decide today. The decision we all need to make is whether we will live forever in Heaven or Hell. (*Isaiah 55:6 Seek the Lord while he may be found; call upon him while he is near*)

Hell is real and I certainly do not want you to end up there! It is more terrible than we can imagine. There is eternal fire, utter darkness, weeping and gnashing of teeth, and being cut to pieces. It is a place of punishment, everlasting destruction and complete alienation from God for all eternity. It is a place of conscious, eternal torment with unending suffering and pain where there is no escape. It is a place where God's wrath will be poured out onto those who have sinned against Him and have not repented. You do NOT want to go to Hell!

On the other hand, Heaven is a place where we will reside in real physical bodies, and where we will experience ultimate peace, everlasting joy, rewards and treasures, and live in the presence of God.

There will be no evil, no pain, no suffering, no worry, no sickness, no crying, no pride, no insecurity, no jealousy, no discrimination, and a perfect relationship with God and all the fellow believers in Heaven with you.

We all break God's law (the Ten Commandments) – that's called sin. It is our sin that builds a wall too high to climb between us and God. Our sin keeps us serving satan whether we have knowingly chosen that or not. It dooms us to an eternity in Hell. The sentence for breaking God's law is going to hell. Romans 6:23 says "for the wages of sin is death …. ", and friend, that's where everyone is headed if they don't repent. There is nothing that we can do to earn our way out of that reality. We can't just be better people or give to the poor or help old ladies or work at an animal shelter or…… All those things are good things, but they won't earn you a place in Heaven.

This is why we all need a savior. We need someone who can remove that wall of sin. That's who Jesus is. Romans 6:23 goes on to say, "… but the free gift of God is eternal life in Christ Jesus our Lord." Jesus stepped into the courtroom and paid your fine. Jesus took your sentence. It is a gift He willingly gives to us free of charge. He is the only one who can remove that wall and give us complete access to God, but we need to ask Him to do it. We need to acknowledge that our behaviors are against God and actually want to change.

W all serve a god, whether it is THE GOD or another god. If you are not serving THE GOD in your daily life, then you are serving the enemy – the evil one – satan. It's one lane or the other. You are either for Him or against Him. *("Whoever is not with me is against me, and whoever does not gather with me scatters" Luke 11:23, Matthew 12:30.)* The choice is yours. Time is running out. Tomorrow is not guaranteed. I pray that everyone reading this can feel God's calling and choose Him as their Lord and Savior!

If this all makes sense and you believe that Jesus is Lord, then I encourage you to talk to God. Invite Him into your life. God doesn't just barge in uninvited. You have to open the door and invite Him in. Are you ready to do that? Then pray with me.

> God, I believe that You are the creator of everything. I believe that You sent Your son Jesus Christ to die on the cross for my sins. I know I have sinned against You, and I am so sorry. Please forgive me. Please send Your Holy Spirit to be with me and guide me as I learn more about You and how to live a life that is pleasing to You. In Jesus name I pray. Amen.

Printed in the United States
by Baker & Taylor Publisher Services